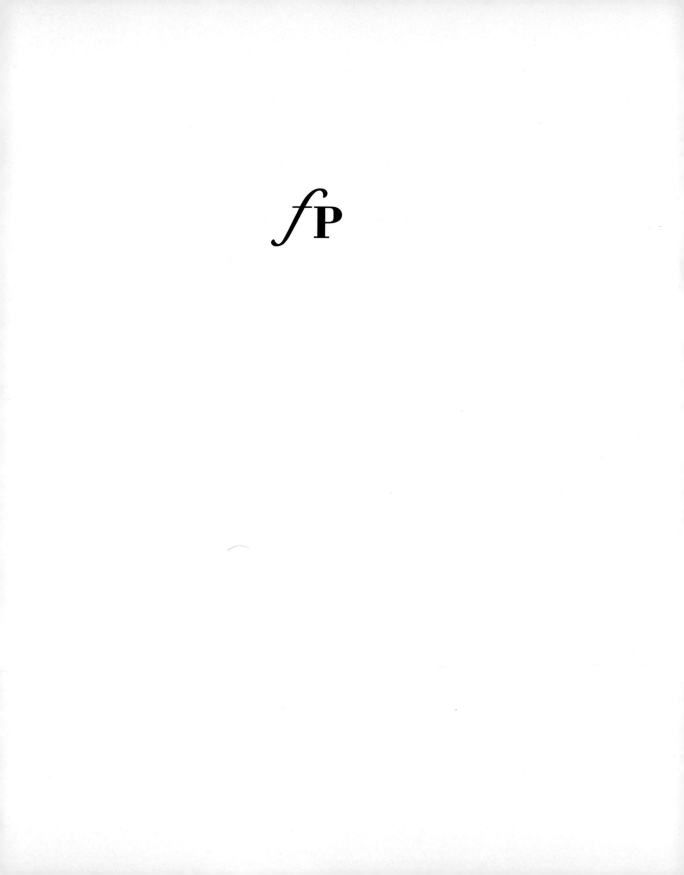

BAKING
WITH THE

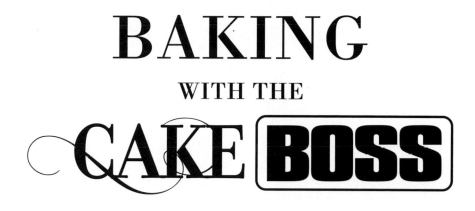

100 of Buddy's Best Recipes and Decorating Secrets

BUDDY VALASTRO

FREE PRESS

New York   London   Toronto   Sydney   New Delhi

*f*P

FREE PRESS
A Division of Simon & Schuster, Inc.
1230 Avenue of the Americas
New York, NY 10020

First Free Press hardcover edition November 2011

FREE PRESS and colophon are trademarks of Simon & Schuster, Inc.

For information about special discounts for bulk purchases,
please contact Simon & Schuster Special Sales at 1-866-506-1949
or business@simonandschuster.com.

The Simon & Schuster Speakers Bureau can bring authors to your live event.
For more information or to book an event contact the Simon & Schuster Speakers Bureau
at 1-866-248-3049 or visit our website at www.simonspeakers.com.

DESIGNED BY ERICH HOBBING

Manufactured in the United States of America

1   3   5   7   9   10   8   6   4   2

Library of Congress Cataloging-in-Publication Data
Valastro, Buddy.
Baking with the Cake boss : 100 of Buddy's best recipes and decorating secrets / Buddy Valastro.
p. cm.
Includes index.
1. Cake. 2. Cake decorating. 3. Carlo's Bake Shop (Hoboken, N.J.) I. Cake boss (Television program) II. Title.
TX771.V335 2011
641.8'653—dc23
2011018216

ISBN 978-1-4391-8352-6
ISBN 978-1-4516-2891-3 (ebook)

To my mother, Mary Valastro.

After Daddy passed away,
you and I promised each other that we would do whatever it took
to keep Carlo's Bake Shop flourishing. We strived, together
with the entire family, to pull that off, and—of course—
the bakery became more successful than ever. In the process,
you became more than a mother to me;
we became best friends.

I talk a lot about how I inherited a lot of Daddy's best traits,
but I was fortunate to receive many of yours as well—
to put it in baking terms, you guys were the recipe
for the man I am today.

And so I dedicate this book to you,
straight from the heart.

Contents

Introduction

It all started with a cookie.

Everything I am professionally. All that I'm capable of doing in a bakery. Every wedding and theme cake I've ever conceived and created. It all began with the first thing I was ever taught to make when I started working at my family's bakery: butter cookies. It's been a long time since my first "official" day on the job—almost twenty-five years—and it *feels* like a long time. When I look back over my life and career, I recall my skills growing at the same slow pace at which a tree grows.

A baker's development doesn't happen overnight. It's a painstaking thing. Even if you have raw talent, you have to nurture it, develop it. You have to patiently back up instinct and intuition with craft and, most of all, practice. Because in baking, practice doesn't just make perfect. Practice also lets you move on to the next level, the next challenge, the next thing to be mastered.

Learning to bake is like learning to speak. You pick up that first word, even if you pronounce it imperfectly, and then pretty soon you learn another, and then another. You might not be able to say every word as clearly as a network anchorman, or put words together into sentences, but even as a kid you know that's where you're headed, to a place where you can string words into sentences, sentences into paragraphs, paragraphs into anything you want—an essay, a story, a memoir—*if* you put in the time to get good at each of the component parts.

It's the same with baking. Those butter cookies were like my first word. They're not difficult to make, and they're still one of the first things we assign to baking newbies at Carlo's Bake Shop, my family's business on Washington Street in Hoboken, New Jersey: You mix a dough of butter, sugar, almond paste, egg whites, and flour; scrape it into a pastry bag; pipe circles of it onto a parchment paper–lined tray; and bake them.

Next to the magnificent theme cakes we produce, those butter cookies might sound like the most idiotproof grunt work you could imagine. But they're not. The beautiful thing about baking is that it all fits together; just as words lead to sentences, and sentences lead to paragraphs, those cookies—as well as the others

I made in my first months on the job—laid the foundation for all the baking and decorating that awaited me, and if you're new to baking, they can do the same thing for you.

THE *KARATE KID* PRINCIPLE

You've probably already made cookies, but I wonder if you have any idea how much you've learned about pastry and cake making from something as simple as mixing and baking a chocolate chip cookie.

If you've made cookies from scratch, then you already have experience with one of the most important things about baking: mixing dough until it's just the way it's supposed to be. As for the baking itself, you've developed an eye and a nose for doneness, and you've learned a little something about how food behaves after it comes out of the oven, like the effect of carryover heat (the way things continue to cook by their own contained heat as they rest), and that the cookies will harden as they cool.

Those things might not seem like much—I bet you've never even given them much thought—but if you've ever made chocolate chip cookies from scratch, then you've already begun to unleash the baker within.

I call this the "*Karate Kid* principle." In the movie *The Karate Kid*—both the original and the 2010 remake—the young protagonist is forced by his master, Mister Miyagi, to execute a series of seemingly mundane tasks: sanding the floor, painting a house, and waxing a car (in the original) or picking up and putting on a jacket, then taking it off and hanging it up (in the remake). The boy doesn't see the value of these tasks—in fact, he thinks the old man is toying with him—but when it comes time to step up and do some real karate, he finds that he knows all he needs to know: the brushstrokes he used to paint taught him the motion for blocking a blow; bending over to pick up the jacket prepared him to duck; and so on. He's been learning more than he ever realized just by doing those simple little things, over and over.

It's the same with baking: You do small tasks like mixing cookie dough, or piping an éclair full of cream, or rolling out rugelach. It's assembly line work, or at least that's how it seems. But when it comes time to do more intricate baking and decorating, you realize you already know a lot of what's required. If you do enough baking, then you don't even have to think about it because your senses take over: Your fingers know what dough should feel like when you work it; your eyes and nose develop a sixth sense for doneness; and your brain makes adjustments based on the end result so you can correct your course the next time to make it even better.

Once you get all those tasks down to a T, and you move on to the next ones, that's when you have your *Karate Kid* moment. All of those cookie-making skills come into play when you decide to tackle pastry; the mixing, rolling, shaping, and baking have become second nature, so you can save your mental energy for what's new: assembly and decorating. And by the time you get to cake making and decorating, and discover that you've already got the tools to do that . . . well, it's a truly mystical moment in a baker's life when we realize that we possess the skills necessary to make our tools and ingredients do whatever we want them to, and that we're capable of more than we ever thought possible. I hope that this book will help you attain such a moment in your own baking life.

I'm living proof of what I'm talking about. In my early days at Carlo's Bake Shop, I was confined to simple baking tasks such as making cookies and what we call "finishing work," which means slicing and piping pastries full of cream, or topping them with maraschino cherries or strawberry halves. Those jobs didn't seem like much at the time, just your basic dues-paying labor. But eventually, I got so good at these rudimentary tasks that I didn't even have to think about them. By making cookies, I learned how to mix, picked up some simple piping techniques, and honed my eye for doneness, learning to discern the fine lines between "hot," "done," and "burned," which were different for each cookie. By making pastry, I learned a greater variety of skills, developed greater finesse with dough, and began to develop what we call the "Hand of the Bag," the oneness with a pastry bag that you need to be able to decorate cakes. And cakes were the next step in my education.

Because repetition leads to mastery, my favorite times at the bakery were the holidays, when we'd bang out 150 pans of éclairs and 150 of cream puffs in a single day. I used to look forward to those crunch times, because when each one was over, my skills had risen to a new level and I was ready to move on to the next thing. January didn't bring just the new year; on the heels of the December madness at Carlo's, it also brought me new challenges in the kitchen.

I've designed this book to track the same path I took at Carlo's, the one that any young baker still takes there today. Of course, you don't have to bake these recipes in the order I've arranged them in this book, especially if you already have a certain degree of baking and decorating experience. But if you do bake them one after the other, in order—and if you take the time to really learn each recipe until it's second nature to you—when you get to the theme cake recipes, you'll be amazed at how much you know: You will be an expert mixer, and baking will be a breeze. If you are going to use fondant, you'll have already developed crucial rolling skills; and if you're going to do a lot of piping, you'll already know all the techniques required to produce the various effects.

YOUR CARLO'S BAKE SHOP APPRENTICESHIP

To put all of this another way: Think of this book as your own, private apprenticeship alongside me, the Cake Boss himself. I am going to teach you everything I learned at my family's bakery, in the same order I learned it. We're going to start by making cookies, then work our way up through the Carlo's "curriculum" of pastries, pies, basic cake decorating, and theme cakes.

There is going to be a difference between my education and yours, however: I'm not going to make you wait for the larger lessons to reveal themselves. As we take on each recipe in this book, I'll tell you exactly how it will help you with future recipes, so you can flip or think ahead and start to connect the dots for yourself.

Of course, if you already have some baking experience—or even if you don't—you don't have to follow my suggested sequence. You can make all of the recipes in this book without cross-referencing any others in the book, except for the occasional "subrecipe" for a filling, icing, or dough. But if you're starting to bake from scratch, I'd encourage you to confine yourself to cookies for a while, then move on to pastries, then pies, and finally to cakes.

THE PEP TALK

Before we get started, I'm going to give you a little talk I like to give to everybody who comes to work with me and my family. Baking is hard work, and in a professional kitchen, it's a team effort. So I think of myself as a coach, and part of my job is to motivate people whenever I can, starting with their first day on the job.

So imagine that it's six o'clock in the morning. You've been up since five. You took a quick shower, pulled on your checkered pants and cook's whites, drove or trained it to Hoboken, and made your way through the predawn streets to the cobblestone alleyway that leads to our back door. You push it open and prepare to step through the looking glass, into your baking future.

The first thing that hits you is the glare. The kitchen is bright. It has to be. We need to be able to discern all the little differences in batters and doughs as they're mixed and in the wide variety of final products as they come out of the ovens.

You spot me waiting for you. Even after all these years, I still love these early morning hours and I'm a bundle of energy and excitement. I take pride in being up and about and hard at work while most of the world is still fast asleep. Most bakers I know feel the same way. These hours are sacred—the streets beyond the bakery walls are quiet; the phones aren't ringing yet. It's the perfect time to commune with our ingredients and our ovens with zero outside distraction. It's the perfect time to bake.

"Hey, how's it going?" I say and we do a high five that turns into a handshake in midair. "Are you ready to *work*?"

"Yes," you say . . . if you know what's good for you.

"That's what we like to hear," I say. "But before we get you started, let's have a cup of coffee."

We head out to the retail floor and help ourselves to two coffees from the pot behind the counter. On the way back into the kitchen, we pass the picture of my father—Buddy Sr.—hanging over the staircase. The words "Gone But Not Forgotten" arc emblazoned across it. And it's true: To this day, his spirit imbues everything we do. His passion and energy inspire everybody who works here—the veterans worked shoulder-to-shoulder with him and the younger generation receives his passion indirectly from the veterans. It's a chain, a continuum, that I hope will never end.

We find a corner of a bench (wooden worktable) where we aren't in anybody's way. As the bakers mix and roll all around us, heaving huge trays of this and that into the ovens, then hauling them out, golden-brown and smelling of sugar and spices, I tell you what I want every new baker to know.

"Within these walls is everything you need to know to be a *complete* baker." When I say "complete," I emphasize the word so much that you jump a little. "Complete baker" is a term that has special meaning at Carlo's. Everybody who works here takes pride in being a complete baker.

"My cake education was nothing special back when I was a kid," I say. "In those days, everybody in a bakery knew how to do everything. 'All-around bakers,' we called ourselves. *Thoroughbreds.* There was nothing that we couldn't do. We baked Tuesday, Wednesday, and Thursday, making everything from biscotti to cakes. Then on Friday, Saturday, and Sunday, when people had their celebrations, we decorated cakes from sunup to dusk.

"Age might be a strike against you in the corporate world," I tell you. "But here, there has always been great respect for the elders, because they've been doing things longer than the rest of us and for the most part are better."

You nod. You look around, and notice that older guys like Danny Dragone—one of our longtime utility players—have no trouble keeping pace with younger guys like my brother-in-law Joey Faugno, who runs the baking department. Both of them are much more than bakers, or even managers; they are fonts of baking knowledge and wisdom. They spend a good part of each and every day patiently nurturing young talent by pointing out the things that their charges can learn only through firsthand baking experience, like calling their attention to the distinct textures and colors that let you know when each dough is done mixing. Or how certain cookies need to finish baking out of the oven, on their pan, even though they might seem a little raw. Or that you need to smell the fresh ricotta we still get from a local farm—in pails, on ice, with no labels or expiration dates—before making cannoli cream, to make sure it's not spoiled. We also check up on our young colleagues in more subtle ways—for example, when I see somebody making a wheat pie, I always take a sniff of the filling as it cooks on the stovetop because my nose will tell me whether or not they remembered to include the orange and lemon zest, both of which give off a distinct and potent perfume.

The old pros look so good doing their jobs that new kids can be intimidated and make bad decisions. While I was writing this book, a pair of young bakers burned two racks of cookies. Not burned black, but burned enough that they weren't right to sell. That's a mistake that anybody can make, even me, even today. What matters isn't whether cookies burn, but what you do with them when that happens. In this case, the guys—maybe afraid we'd be cross with them—put the cookies with the properly baked ones that were headed for the pastry cases on the retail floor, which was a big mistake. Fortunately, we caught the burned ones before they went out for sale. They weren't so horribly wrong that they had to end up in the garbage can, but we couldn't sell them, so we donated them to the homeless, which is what we do with the baked goods we produce that aren't quite up to our commercial standards, but are still pretty delicious.

Joey, Danny, and all the other veteran bakers are each like well-oiled machines in their own right. And there's no chit-chat, no clowning around—they are all focused on what they are doing, and on doing it to the best of their ability. One guy might be mixing batch after batch of dough, which we still do in an old industrial Hobart mixer, the baker rolling up his sleeve and sticking his arm down into the depths of the bowl to scrape it; another might be pulling trays off the rotating shelves in the oven, then getting trays of unbaked cookies and pastries onto those shelves before too much heat has escaped; yet another might be doing finishing work, icing cookies or piping éclairs full of cream.

I think about how each of these guys could switch roles or how they could all do the same task if that's what the production day called for. It's an increasingly rare way of doing things.

"Times have changed," I say. "This is the era of specialization. Today, there are guys who just bake, and guys who just decorate. But I think it's best to do it all."

And this is when I look up from my coffee and stare you right in the eye: "That's how we're going to train *you*."

This is also about the time I can tell that a new baker is ready to get going, to get his hands dusty with flour and start making the magic happen. But before I set that person to work, I like to make a few more points, and I want to make them to you before *we* begin baking together.

1. Success in baking is founded on repetition. The most important thing to realize about baking is that repetition is the gateway to greatness. Just as athletes have to train and musicians have to practice, if you want to be a terrific baker, you need to learn to love the process— from measuring out your ingredients to mixing batters and dough to baking to decorating. There's no separating one part from another, because all those steps add up to success in the final product, and if any one of them is suspect, then the whole thing falls apart. I also think of great bakers as soldiers, because it's all about discipline, about taking great pride in turning yourself into a human machine that can execute the same series of steps over and over in the exactly same way.

2. There are many ways to be creative. On *Cake Boss*, the theme cakes are the center of attention, and with good reason: They are jaw-dropping, showstopping examples of unbridled creativity. Our theme cakes make anybody who sees them, even other professionals, say, "How did they do *that*?" But there are many ways of being creative. If you don't have the hands for, or interest in, elaborate decorating, but love the flavors and textures of delicious baked goods—and the pleasure those qualities give to the people you bake for—then you might turn out to have a skill for creating your own distinct recipes. Or you might find that you have a knack for instituting small changes that make a big impact, like adapting my recipe for Raspberry Bars (page 113) to make apricot, blueberry, or lemon-orange bars; or perhaps making a simple but attention-getting adjustment like dipping half of each bar in chocolate. Or you might take the recipe for Butterflies (page 97) and relocate the wings from the top to the bottom, using them as legs to fashion a different animal, bringing your own distinct sense of play to the pastry.

In other words, don't feel that you have to become a cake boss yourself in order to find happiness in baking; there are countless home bakers out there who take great pride and satisfaction in making nothing but cookies. If that's where your comfort zone and happiness lie, be happy with that and get as good at it as you possibly can.

3. Always be willing to try new things. As much as I believe in repetition and consistency, I also believe that it's important to try new things, to balance the required discipline for baking with a chance to be spontaneous and to grow. Whether it's tinkering with a tried-and-true recipe to see if you can make it even better, or attempting to design something you've never seen before, it's worth the trouble and relatively minor expense to innovate, especially if you end up bringing a new recipe or design into the world.

4. No two bakers are exactly alike. There's no one way to do anything when it comes to baking. The recipes and advice I share work for me, and for my family and coworkers, and for the customers who line up outside our shop on Washington Street in Hoboken, New Jersey. But—who knows?—you might come up with a new way of doing things—from tweaking a recipe to discovering a new use for a kitchen tool—that works for you. At the end of the day, baking is about your own individualistic relationship with the tools and ingredients; if you can come up with your own way of doing something, don't hesitate to go give it a try. And if you change a recipe, be sure to keep notes on what you did so you can do it again! (See "Keeping a Book," below.)

5. Believe. Along with a good rolling pin and mixer, and a well-stocked pantry, there's something else you need every time you bake: confidence. If you watch seasoned bakers do their thing, they all exude an easy confidence. You need to have the same slight swagger when you step up to your workstation and dust it with flour. You need to know in your bones that you will not fail. Why is this so important? Because you need to trust all your senses; for example, most dough doesn't look anything like what the final product it produces looks like, so you need to have the confidence to know you've mixed it properly. Similarly, when you step up to a naked cake, piping bag in hand, and get ready to go to work on that blank canvas, if you have any doubt in yourself, it will be reflected in imperfect borders and wavy lines. Believe in yourself when you bake and decorate; it's as important as anything else.

KEEPING A BOOK

All professional bakers keep a notebook full of hard-won baking wisdom—everything from recipes for the signature items in the shop where they work to old family treasures they want to be sure survive through the ages. But you can't necessarily pick up a baker's book and use it like a cookbook, because a lot of us, especially the veterans, keep our notes in a form of code, changing at least one ingredient so that nobody can steal from us.

My favorite story about this tradition involves one of the legends of Carlo's Bake Shop, Mike Vernola, better known as Old Man Mike. Mike's encrypted recipes were almost as revered as the man himself. To keep a young, up-and-coming baker from ripping off his secrets, Mike always changed the quantity of one ingredient in a recipe; for instance, an ounce of salt might be represented as twelve ounces of salt. There was no rhyme or reason to it; one recipe would have the flour wrong, another the sugar. And only Mike knew the correct quantities.

One day, a job applicant was trying out with us, and he managed to get his hands on Mike's book. Somebody saw him take it into the bathroom, and—worried that Mike's intellectual property was being lifted—reported it to me. I tracked down my father with great urgency and reported what was going on. Rather than freak out, he let loose with a roar of laughter.

"What's so funny?" I asked.

"He's got *Mike's* book," my father said. "Nothing's written down right. He won't be able to use any of it!"

Now, that's a funny story, but—in all seriousness—I encourage you to keep your own book. At the very least, you should keep notes in the margins of this and other cookbooks. Maybe you like a little more sugar than I do for a sweeter effect in some recipes; or maybe your oven is a little slower (or faster) than mine, so you want to adjust baking times. Maybe you like to add another spice or chocolate chips to some recipes, or maybe you want to remember to make a dish for a particular person or occasion. Write those things down, *all* of those things.

If you do a lot of baking, especially if you're a professional or aspiring professional, you should go beyond making notes in a book and start keeping your own notebook. Make it something personal that fits comfortably into your bag or your pocket. Keep notes (they can be shorthand) on recipes, tricks, lessons, and so on. And do yourself a favor: Periodically type those notes up and keep them in a backed-up computer file so that you have them available if you lose the notebook. If you come up with a lot of original stuff, you might even do what the old-timers do and write in code; just be sure you remember what you changed so you can use the recipes yourself!

Getting Started:
A Tour of the Kitchen

When a new kid shows up at Carlo's Bake Shop, ready to learn and to work, positively *smelling* of eagerness, I feel the same way I do when I begin designing a cake: that anything is possible, that—with the proper guidance—he can go as far as he wants. I want you to have the same mind-set as one of those kids as we begin baking and decorating together.

The first thing we do when a new baker shows up is give him a tour of the kitchen. You might think that we'd skip this step here, since you're working in your own home kitchen. But there are things from my world that you can apply to yours.

ORGANIZATION

Amazingly, people almost never bump into each other at Carlo's Bake Shop. Even when the place is at its busiest—Easter weekend or the day before Christmas—when it's all hands on deck and every employee is working day and night, the orchestration of people, ingredients, trays of pastries, and specialty cakes is neat and orderly.

The reason for this is organization. Our kitchen is set up for the most efficient and—dare I say it—*elegant* flow of people.

You're probably the only person in your kitchen when you bake, but let me tell you something: You can get in your own way if you don't set up your kitchen correctly. Of course we all have unique configurations and different amounts of space to work with, but here are a few general suggestions.

1. *Work area.* If possible, dedicate some counter space to prep work, which is the preliminary work that takes place before the actual baking: chopping, mixing, rolling, and so on. You'll want some coun-

ter space (or table space) where you can keep your basic equipment, which in the case of baking is the rolling pin, mixer, measuring spoons and cups, spatulas, and so on. If there are drawers beneath or above this area, that's where you want to have your parchment paper and plastic wrap. The ideal scenario is that once you've gathered your ingredients from the fridge and pantry, you can do all your mixing, rolling, and other tasks without moving from one spot.

2. *Keep the sink and stove areas clear.* If at all possible, keep the counter space closest to your oven and sink free and clear and—just as important—*clean.* Why? Because you are constantly setting things next to the sink, or removing things from the oven, or adding things to a pot on the stovetop, so counter space is precious. Don't store things there if you don't have to.

3. *Storage.* Keep all your dry goods for baking in one place: sugar, flour, baking powder, baking soda. You might even consider keeping two containers of salt in your kitchen: one in your baking area and one closer to the stove. This way, you can gather all your ingredients swiftly. It also makes it easy to prepare a shopping list because you can take a quick inventory without having to search all over your kitchen to find out what you have and don't have; you can just calmly check your baking area and see what needs replenishing.

4. *Baking equipment.* Equipment such as pans, mixing bowls, and the like doesn't need to be stored right next to your prep area. In fact, I suggest storing these near your dishwasher or drying rack, because that's the last place they'll be before you put them away.

Equipment

These are the pieces of equipment and tools that you should have on hand if you plan to do a variety of baking with any kind of regularity. For tools exclusively needed for cakes and cupcakes see the list on page 15.

ALL-PURPOSE COOKWARE

BAKING PANS AND TRAYS

Baking trays are a great example of my belief that everything matters in a kitchen—they aren't just vessels that hold things during baking; they are a factor in how evenly and controlled the baking process is. I'm not going to name names, but when I visit people's homes, I'm sometimes shocked that people who have otherwise top-notch kitchens treat their baking pans as an afterthought, using paper-thin aluminum trays, sometimes crusted with baked-on food. These don't conduct heat evenly, and cooked-on food will throw smoke in a hot oven. (And that smoke will contaminate whatever you're baking with unwanted flavor.)

I suggest you have at least four pans: two regular 13 by 9-inch pans and two nonstick. If you don't want to buy a nonstick pan, you can purchase a Silpat, a silicone liner that can be laid over the pan. (For a 13 by 9-inch baking tray, you want a Petit Jelly Roll Silpat measuring 11¾ by 8¼ inches.) I recommend that you purchase pans with some kind of rim because you will need it for some recipes, and even when you don't need it, there's no harm in having it there. (The rim also makes a pan easier to grab.) The pans should be made of heavy-gauge metal and be light rather than dark in color (dark material tends to hasten burning), and you should keep them clean by scrubbing with warm, sudsy water; use steel wool on the regular pan and a soft sponge on the nonstick.

COOKIE SHEETS

Similar to my suggested specs for baking trays, cookie sheets should be medium to heavy weight and light in color but also—this is important—rimless, so that heat can evenly bathe the cookies as they bake. (Some sheets have a sloping end that makes it easier to grab them, and to slide cookies off the tray and onto a rack, and that's fine.) Rimless pans don't just allow for better airflow; they also make it easier to check on cookies when they bake, allowing ease of access with a spatula. (At Carlo's, where our oven has rotating shelves, the pans themselves basically circulate, so we use rimmed baking trays for just about everything.) A good, readily available size cookie sheet is 17 by 14 inches, although other sizes are fine so long as they fit in your oven without blocking the flow of air from top to bottom.

MINI MUFFIN TRAY

For making Rum Babas (page 103) and Butterflies (page 97), a nonstick mini muffin tray with 24 wells is essential.

PIE PANS

Most of the pies in this book are made in a 9-inch pan. Two notable exceptions are the *Frutti di Bosco* on page 145, which calls for a fluted tart pan, and the wheat pie on page 137, which calls for a 10-inch pie pan.

DOUBLE BOILER

A double boiler, which keeps heat from coming into direct contact with the bottom of a pot, is the smart choice to use for melting chocolate and making icing, and for keeping them warm without the risk of scorching them. If you don't have a double boiler, you can set a metal or heatproof glass bowl (such as Pyrex) on top of a pot of simmering water; just be sure the bowl completely seals the top of the pot so steam and heat don't escape, causing the water to evaporate. Sealing is hard to do, and you risk giving yourself a steam burn, so if you plan to make recipes that call for a double boiler, just invest in one rather than using a makeshift one. You'll use your double boiler for nonbaking recipes, too, eventually.

FOR CAKES AND CUPCAKES

CAKE PANS

At home, I generally use a 9 by 2-inch round cake pan. Since many of the cake recipes in this book produce two 9-inch cakes, you'll want to have two pans for baking out of this book. If you plan to make the chiffon cakes on pages 300 to 303, you will need two 7-inch round cake pans.

I like aluminum pans. I know that springform pans are popular, but I don't care for them because they're harder to clean and they're really not necessary. If you grease and flour a pan correctly (see page 297) and let it cool, it will unmold just fine.

If you plan to make the Thanksgiving cake (page 255) you will also need a Bundt or Bundt-style form (8 inches in diameter and 3 inches deep). For square and rectangular cakes, you need to use a 13 by 9 by 2-inch-deep pan, and for the Valentine's Day Cake (page 219) and Santa Christmas Cake (page 275), you will need two heart-shaped molds.

CUPCAKE TRAY

For making cupcakes you will need two nonstick cupcake trays with 12 wells each. If you have only cupcake pans that are not nonstick, grease with butter, nonstick spray, or vegetable shortening before baking.

TURNTABLE

A turntable is a positively indispensable piece of equipment for frosting and decorating cakes. For more about this see page 152.

TOOLS

BRUSHES

I recommend that you have three types of brushes as part of your kitchen arsenal.

A pastry brush is the best way to apply syrups and other soaking liquids to sponge cakes, to work with melted butter, and to apply water to fondant if you don't have a water pen (see page 195). (A squeeze bottle with a sponge tip applicator or a spray bottle will also work.)

A bench brush has long, stiff bristles and is made for sweeping flour off your work surface. I rarely see these in home kitchens, but I recommend you own one because it makes it very easy to get your surface clean.

A large makeup brush, sometimes called a powder brush, is useful for patting down sugar or cornstarch on your work surface when you are working with fondant. Use it to get any lumps or clumps out of the sugar or cornstarch, whether on your work surface or on the fondant itself.

MICROPLANE ZESTER

In the old days at Carlo's we made our lemon zest by rubbing lemons on one of those old-fashioned box graters. It wasn't the best way to go—the now-familiar recipe instruction not to shave off any bitter pith with your grater wasn't even on our mind—but we didn't know any better. (We also had to garbage the occasional batch when a guy grated a little of his knuckle into the bowl along with the rind!) Then along came the Microplane zester. It's a common kitchen tool today, but was originally devised as a woodworking tool. It's got dozens of minirazors that produce a snowy zest from lemons, oranges, and other citrus fruits.

MIXING BOWLS

Ceramic and glass mixing bowls are perfectly fine options, but I prefer stainless steel for a very practical reason: They don't break if you drop them. Get yourself a good assortment of mixing bowl sizes—generally speaking, I like to use a bowl that's large for a given task because it helps keep ingredients from splashing or flying out of the bowl when you whisk or stir.

PARCHMENT PAPER

Always have some parchment paper on hand: You will use it to line baking and cookie sheets for a variety of items, and I often use a parchment pencil (see page 185) for decorating pastries, pies, and cakes. By the way, if you've ever wondered why some recipes call for parchment paper and some don't, it's almost always a matter of preventing what you're baking from sticking to the bottom of the pan. Parchment can sometimes be left out if you're baking a batter with a high fat content, because it will release just enough fat to keep itself from sticking. (In this book, I don't use parchment in these cases.) Whatever you do, if you don't have parchment paper, don't substitute waxed paper instead. Waxed paper smokes like crazy and will fill your oven and kitchen with that smoke and set off your smoke detector.

PASTRY BAGS

The pastry bag is one of the most important tools for a baker. At Carlo's and in this book, it is are used for everything from piping out cookie dough to filling pastries to icing and decorating cakes.

There are four main types of bag: polyurethane, canvas, disposable, and makeshift. I don't necessarily favor one over the other; instead, I like different bags for different jobs.

For piping cookie dough and thick, heavy batters, the gold standard is a canvas bag, because of its durability. You can really squeeze it, using as much pressure as you like or need to, without fear of busting it open.

For decorating and piping with buttercream, I prefer a polyurethane bag because I find it lets you feel closer to the cream, giving you a greater sense of control.

If you're working with anything that will stain a polyurethane bag, disposable pastry bags are perfectly acceptable to use instead. For example, dark buttercreams such as black, red, and green will all stain a bag, so I recommend a disposable bag for working with them.

A makeshift bag isn't really an "official" type of bag, but it can be a lifesaver if you don't have a bag on hand and want to do something that requires it. You can fashion a makeshift bag by using a large (1- or 2-gallon) resealable plastic bag: Fill it with whatever you'll be piping, fold the top closed, and snip off a corner to act as the "tip." You can't get much finesse with a makeshift bag, but it's a perfectly viable way of frosting a cake, filling cannoli, icing cupcakes, and applying meringue to a pie.

A note about working with pastry bags: When you are working with meringue, buttercream, and other sensitive mixtures, the temperature of your hands can cause what's in the bag to soften. Different people's hands have different temperatures; mine, for example, tend to generate heat, so after ten minutes of piping, I often squeeze out whatever's left in the bag, then refill the bag with more of whatever I'm piping. If your hands run hot, you may need to do the same.

PASTRY BAG TIPS

At the very least, you should have a #6 plain and a #7 star pastry tip for piping cream, frostings, and fillings. For decorating cakes and cupcakes, a good set of interchangeable decorating tips is essential. There are many sets on the market that feature a variety of tips; you might want to purchase one, or you can amass a collection as you bake more and more recipes, but always check before embarking on a new recipe to be sure you have the necessary tips. You can purchase them individually if necessary, or if you don't want to buy a whole set right off.

Interchangeable tips are small tips shaped to produce specific effects, such as grass, leaves, or the shape that mimics rose petals. You affix these to pastry bags with a coupler that acts as a dock or port for them. In addition to empowering you to create visual effects, tips and bags are also convenient: If you need to create different effects with the same color icing, you don't need to fill different bags; you just change the tip. Throughout the book, I indicate when an interchangeable tip is called for; if a recipe does not indicate "interchangeable," then you just drop the desired tip (a regular pastry tip) into the bag before filling it with the desired filling or frosting.

RACKS

You should have at least two racks for cooling cookies and pastries after baking. (If space on your counter is limited, or you want to avoid resting hot trays on it, you can let the trays cool on top of the racks until the cookies are ready to be transferred.) Racks are available in a variety of sizes; I recommend having at least two nonstick racks, 17 by 12 inches each, which is toward the larger end of the size spectrum.

ROLLING PIN

Everybody in the kitchen at Carlo's has his or her own opinion about rolling pins. There are only two main types of pin (three, if you count polyurethane), but we're as personal about them as a hustler is about his pool stick. Both wooden and marble pins are fine; the overall weight and balance are more important than the material. For rolling out cookie dough, pie crust, and raspberry bars, I like a straight wooden rolling pin. (In reality, I leaned to roll those items with a broomstick, but you don't want to do that at home!) For tougher jobs, such as rolling out rugelach, *pasta frolla* to stripe a wheat pie, or puff pastry dough, a wooden, steel, or marble pin with ball bearings that allow the cylinder to spin is better. Those ball bearings help a spinning pin make its way through denser dough. (But I generally use a wooden pin here as well. I've done it so many times that I'm comfortable with it.)

For rolling fondant, I recommend a polyurethane rolling pin because it stays at a good neutral temperature and has a terrific weight for pressing out the fondant, which can become uneven. You don't want to use wood for fondant because wooden rolling pins tend to develop little divots over time, and these will get imprinted into the fondant.

SCALES

Some ingredients are measured by weight rather than volume, so if you don't already own one, I suggest purchasing a kitchen scale. Digital battery-operated scales can be purchased for about $20 and many are small enough to tuck away in a drawer or cupboard when not in use.

SCRAPER

In a home kitchen, a rubber spatula fills in for most of the things we use plastic scrapers for in a professional bakery, namely folding ingredients together and scraping mixtures out of a bowl or a pot. But I still recommend owning a plastic scraper because a spatula keeps you at a bit of a remove from the food you're working with, and sometimes you want to have a greater feeling of control.

In our kitchen at Carlo's, we also use a metal scraper for scraping our benches (wooden work tables), especially for removing caked-on flour. But I don't recommend this tool at home because so many home kitchen surfaces are delicate or prone to scratching.

SIFTER

For ensuring the even distribution of leavening agents such as baking soda and baking powder, and loosening up compacted flour and other ingredients, a sifter is essential. If you don't yet have a sifter and are dying to get started, in its place you can pour your ingredients into a fine-mesh strainer and gently shake it over the bowl into which you are sifting, but the result won't be as fine.

SPATULAS

The three types of spatula called for throughout this book are so different that it seems odd to call them by the same name.

Cookie spatula or pancake spatula: This is probably the first spatula you ever heard of, meant for lifting baked goods out of pans or turning cookies or pancakes as they cook. Sometimes also called a "turner," it's the one we use for checking doneness on cookies and pastries and for lifting them out of their pans.

Icing spatula: Many baking books recommend an offset spatula (aka angled spatula) for icing cakes, but I like a plain old flat icing spatula (we call it a "bow knife" in the Carlo's kitchen), which gives you a greater feeling of control because of its straight shape. I like an 8-inch icing spatula, which I find works well for any task.

Rubber or silicone spatula: This common kitchen tool gets used a lot in baking, mainly for folding two mixtures together or for scraping mixtures out of bowls. It's a good idea to have a set that includes small, medium, and large spatulas in order to be able to accommodate any size job.

STAND MIXER

If you can afford it and have the room for it on your counter, there is simply nothing better for mixing than a good, sturdy stand mixer, which is basically a miniature version of the mammoth industrial mixers we use at Carlo's. You'll need the paddle, whip, and hook attachments.

If you don't have a stand mixer, you can also use a hand mixer for many recipes (I've indicated which ones in the book), but the motors aren't generally as powerful as those on a stand mixer and your arm isn't as durable as the stand itself, so you'll need to take the time to let ingredients such as butter, cream cheese, and shortening really soften before you begin mixing with a hand mixer.

If you do use a hand mixer, set a damp kitchen towel under the mixing bowl to hold it in place. It's a tried-and-true trick that makes mixing much easier than trying to mix with one hand while holding the bowl with the other, especially if you have to pour or drizzle liquids into the bowl while mixing.

In some of these recipes, you can simply use your hands to mix. I'll tell you when that's the best way. Just make sure that your hands are immaculately clean before using them.

THERMOMETERS

For checking the temperature of batters and buttercream, a kitchen thermometer is the only way to go. I suggest that you take advantage of modern technology and purchase an instant-read thermometer that gives you quick, exact, digital information.

It's a good idea to have an oven thermometer to be sure you're baking at the right temperature. Even if your oven reads correctly today, it might begin to run a little hot or a little cold over time. Position your oven thermometer on the same rack you'll be baking on, which will almost always be the center rack.

TIMER

Don't rely on your memory in the kitchen; it's a recipe for disaster. ("Did I put the cake in the oven at 5:45, or was it 5:54?") Get a timer. In particular, I recommend a timer with at least two clocks in case you're doing more than one thing at a time.

WHISK(S)

It's a good idea to have a large and a small whisk on hand for beating mixtures of varying sizes by hand.

WOODEN SPOON(S)

For stirring mixtures as they cook, a wooden spoon or two should be a part of any kitchen arsenal.

Notes on Ingredients

You are no doubt already familiar with most of the ingredients called for in baking. But I wanted to share some of my tips and advice for shopping for and storing them, and for selecting the best options for each baked good.

BUTTER

The recipes in this book use unsalted (sweet) butter. If you like, use organic butter, though it's by no means essential. By the way, butter is a sponge for other flavors in your refrigerator; that's why there's a little butter drawer built into the door of most fridges. But that door isn't exactly airtight; keep your butter wrapped in plastic wrap, and freeze any sticks that you won't be using for a while. You don't want cheese or smoked meat or onion smells that get in your butter to get in your cookies or cakes.

COCOA AND CHOCOLATE

News flash: the rich chocolate flavor in chocolate cakes and other baked goods comes not from chocolate but from cocoa. Of all the ingredients you're going to use in your baking, the place where it pays to invest the most, I think, is cocoa. Buy the best you can find and afford. At Carlo's Bake Shop we use Callebaut. (Valrhona is also terrific.) Regardless of brand, choose a Dutch-process cocoa that has a 22 to 24% fat content, which offers the most concentrated flavor.

As for chocolate, I like to keep a good supply of chocolate chips on hand, even for recipes in which chocolate is melted, because starting with chips saves you from having to chop up blocks of chocolate before tossing them into the double boiler or microwave.

EGGS

All the recipes in this book call for extra-large eggs. If you have easy access to organic or local, farm-raised eggs, they will make your baking taste better. Believe it or not, eggs are one ingredient that are actually better to bake with when they're older than when they're fresh, although you certainly don't want to use them after their "best by" date. In older eggs, the yolks are firmer, making it easier to separate them from the whites when you need to do that; and the proteins in the whites are more relaxed, making it easier to achieve a frothy result when whipping them. Having your whites at room temperature further relaxes them. So don't feel you have to run out for a fresh half-dozen or dozen eggs every time you want to bake.

If you don't know how old your eggs are, there's an easy way to test if they're still good. Fill a glass or a measuring cup with water and gently place the egg in it. If the egg sinks, it's good. If it floats, that means it has gas in the shell and it's well on its way to going bad. Toss the floaters. But just because one egg in a dozen floats doesn't mean that all of them will, so don't throw out a whole carton if you find just one bad egg.

FLOURS

I know it simplifies things to have just one type of flour in your kitchen, but I am a big believer in the virtues of cake flour and pastry flour. Where possible, I call for all-purpose (unbleached) flour* in my recipes, but in some cases I insist on cake or pastry flour. Here's why.

CAKE FLOUR

Plain and simple, there's a smooth, refined mouthfeel you get with cake flour that just isn't possible with any other type of flour. (It's also not possible with the combination of all-purpose flour and cornstarch that's sometimes substituted for cake flour, so I choose not to include that formula here.) The scientific reason is that cake flour has a lower protein content (8 percent) than any other type of flour. Just run your hands through some all-purpose flour, then through some cake flour, and you'll instantly perceive the difference: All-purpose flour is grainy; cake flour is dense and pleasing—running my fingers through it reminds me of running my fingers through wet sand at the beach. Will the recipes "work" with

*By the way, stay away from self-rising all-purpose flour, which has leavening agents added.

all-purpose flour? In some cases, yes . . . but they won't have the magic we all want in our cakes.

PASTRY FLOUR

The relatively low protein content of pastry flour (about 9 percent) is responsible for the crusty texture of certain cookies and pastries. As with cake flour, you can sometimes substitute all-purpose flour, but the product won't come out the same.

LARD

Back in the day, lard—rendered pork fat—was used in just about every pastry made in a bakery like Carlo's for the simple reason that it was cheaper than vegetable shortening or butter. Today, we use butter more than lard because it has a richer, more refined taste. But I still like lard in some recipes: Nothing makes a cannoli shell crispier than frying it in lard, and lard also imparts that authentic, Italian-American bakery flavor in some recipes.

MARGARINE

I wish I could tell you exactly why we use the butter substitute margarine in some of our recipes, but the truth is that, like so much of what we do at Carlo's, it's just tradition. Certain recipes have used margarine since they came into our repertoire and we continue to make them with margarine in accordance with the "if it ain't broke, don't fix it" principle. I suggest that you use only regular, unsalted sticks of margarine.

MILK

If you have a preference for low- or reduced-fat milk, I respect that, but I encourage you to use whole milk in your baking if at all possible. The final product will taste better, and that fat helps bind the ingredients.

NUTS

Nuts are deceptive ingredients. They seem tough and impenetrable, but in reality, they are among the most sensitive baking ingredients, with a relatively short window of freshness and a tendency to go rancid before you know it. Try to purchase only what you'll use quickly, or keep any extras in plastic bags in the refrigerator or freezer. Before you use them, taste them to check their freshness. A rancid nut doesn't taste like, say, rancid butter or meat; rancid nuts tend to have a slightly fishy taste and odor to them that's just not good. Throw them out for the squirrels or birds.

Whenever you are using nuts in a recipe, it's a good idea to toast them to bring out all their earthy flavor. Toast them in a frying pan over low heat or in a 350°F oven until fragrant, about 10 minutes; whether working on the stovetop or in the oven, shake the pan to ensure even cooking and prevent scorching. Let the nuts cool completely before using them.

SALT

If you're a new baker, you might be surprised to see that some recipes in this book call for salt. That's because salt does for these desserts the same thing it does for savory recipes: It elevates the flavors it comes into contact with. We've upgraded a lot of the ingredients we use at Carlo's over the years, but we still use plain old iodized table salt in the kitchen. What can I tell you? It's tradition. Those eighty-pound bags that are piled up in our stockroom are as much a part of our culture (and of many other bakeries) as the recipes we've been using for generations.

The recipes in this book were tested with table salt, but you can substitute coarse kosher salt, or fine sea salt, if you like—the amounts are so small in these recipes that it won't make a difference.

SUGARS

For sweetening purposes, I usually use granulated sugar, and that's what I mean when I call simply for sugar in my recipes. For a richer, darker flavor, I sometimes use light brown sugar. Powdered sugar (aka confectioners' sugar or 10X sugar) is something I use to make quick icings for black-and-white cookies or pastries like napoleons. (Powdered sugar also makes a cameo in the recipes for the Chocolate Brownie Clusters on page 53 and the Seven-Layer Cookies on page 61.) The only other sugar I call for is crystal sugar, which is a thicker granulated sugar (the clumps are larger) used to add sweetness and color to meringue in a lemon meringue pie.

VANILLA

I'm not kidding when I call for pure vanilla extract in my ingredient lists; stay far, far away from imitation or artificially flavored vanilla. Those imposters simply don't taste like vanilla and their chemical quality can ruin an entire batch of cookies or an otherwise perfectly made cake.

VEGETABLE OIL

Don't substitute canola or other neutral oils for vegetable oil in my recipes because the vegetable oil is already a substitute, a stand-in for the foodservice products that we use at Carlo's but that you can't get at home. You need the fat and viscosity of vegetable oil to attain the desired result in the recipes that call for it.

VEGETABLE SHORTENING

We use vegetable shortening, such as Crisco, in many of our recipes both because it is part of many of our most tried-and-true recipes and because it can take more of a beating than butter. Over the years, I've replaced shortening with butter in some recipes, but in many I replaced only half the shortening because of the stability that shortening provides in the finished product.

The Zone and
How to Get There

Baking is my work, but it's also my retreat, my way of meditating and finding my center. Of course, there are days when we're just trying to keep up with the production schedule at Carlo's, but there are also times when baking—and especially decorating—takes me to another place, a place where I'm removed from the physical world and can take a mental vacation from my troubles. That's what I call "The Zone."

Whether you're a beginner or an experienced home cook, you can get into The Zone, too. The Zone can mean different things to different people, but at the very least, it should mean that baking is a retreat for you, something that's fun and takes you out of your own head.

Here are a few ways to help yourself get to that place.

- *Dress properly.* Obviously, you're not going to wear a professional baker's uniform in your home kitchen, but there is a way to dress for success when baking. Wear comfortable clothing that you don't care too much about (you don't want to stress out if some food gets on your chest or sleeve) and that won't make you feel like an overheated marshmallow when the oven is cranked up. Invest in a good, comfortable pair of light, rubber-soled shoes that give you support and traction, so that you don't slip if there's a spill. Lots of chefs wear clogs or Crocs, but I've been wearing the same make and model of shoes since I started baking, and I just wouldn't feel right in the kitchen without them.
- *Work in a clean, uncluttered environment.* Even if you have a kitchen full of stuff, make some room for yourself to bake. This extends to equipment as well: I love to use oversize mixing bowls because I am less likely to spray flour and liquid around the room when I work in them.
- *Know what you're doing.* Read all recipes (and subrecipes, if there are any) in their entirety before you do anything. If you don't feel you have

a good comfort level before starting to gather your ingredients, read the recipe again. Repeat until you have a mental picture of the "cooking itinerary" that will take you from start to finish.

- *Have the ingredients out and if possible in the order you will use them.* Be sure each one is in the state it's supposed to be in—eggs at room temperature, butter softened or melted. You can even prep your pans by greasing, flouring, and lining them, and so on. Imagine you're on a television cooking show, where all the ingredients are ready to go into a bowl or pan. Along the same lines, be sure you have the right size/material equipment that you need. Even check to be sure you have what you need to store things—plastic wrap, foil, airtight containers, and so forth.

- *Have the oven rack where you want it (usually the middle) before you preheat the oven.* You might also consider removing the other racks, especially those above the rack you'll be using, so you can get things into and out of the oven without worrying about hitting the rack above.

- *Create a mood of solitude and silence.* We've all seen depictions of kitchens full of action and wisecracking bakers and cooks; you might even have seen a little of that on *Cake Boss*. But unless you are a professional whose hands know what they're doing without thinking, I suggest that you bake with no distractions—that means no conversation and no phone calls. (If you're addicted to your BlackBerry, you might even put it in a drawer while you work. This will also protect it from splashes and other damage.) Baking requires constant focus on very subtle details; give it your full attention. The one gray area for me here is music: I don't like music on when I'm measuring, mixing, and prepping, but I love music when I decorate because it helps put me in a mood and get me into a flow.

- *Clean as you go.* Unless you have to keep moving, wash utensils and vessels that you're done with and get them into the dishwasher or drying rack. A cluttered, messy space can have a huge impact on your thinking, reaction time, and overall peace of mind.

- *If you make a mistake, don't become emotionally involved.* As in life, we grow by making mistakes. You are going to make mistakes in baking. Learn from them, do what you can to correct them, and move on.

KITCHEN SAFETY

I'd also like to put in a word for kitchen safety. While I hope that nothing will ever go seriously wrong in your kitchen, it is good to be prepared. Here again is a place where you might learn something from a professional kitchen, where a fire extinguisher is a legal requirement. Keep an extinguisher close by in case of a fire. Baking soda is also a tried and true way of firefighting: Smother the fire with baking soda; in the case of an oven fire, close the door to deprive the fire of oxygen and cause it to die out.

Along these same lines, don't wear anything that can droop or dangle into an open flame or get caught in your mixer, like long, loose sleeves. I don't know why you'd have a necktie on in a kitchen, but if you do, get it outta there. If you have long hair, clamp it up or wear a hat. (You should really wear a hat anyway, just to keep any stray hairs from finding their way into your dough. Or you can do what I do and get it down and back with plenty of hair gel!)

Finally, I love baking with my kids, and love when people tell me they made my recipes with their kids helping out. But *please* don't let your children use any knives or motorized equipment, keep them away from hot ovens, and don't let them in the kitchen unless you are with them and able to keep a close eye on them. I let my kids add things to mixing bowls as long as the bowls are not on a stand mixer, try their hand at rolling with a pin, and punch out shapes with cookie cutters, *and not much else.* Depending on their age, I suggest you limit yours to the same safe tasks.

Basic Baking Techniques

I'll reinforce all of these points the same way we do at Carlo's Bake Shop—through the actual recipes that follow—but I want to emphasize a few things before we start baking.

MEASURING

The most exact way to measure is by weight, and that's the way we do it in professional kitchens. But since most home cooks are used to measuring by volume (for example, teaspoons, tablespoons, and cups), that's how we tested the recipes in this book. (We still call for weights of some ingredients like fondant, though, to help you be as accurate as possible and to help guide your shopping.) To use the right amount of dry ingredients, when using any kind of measure, use a spatula or straight-edged knife to level off the ingredients. You can use your index finger if necessary, but make sure you don't brush out too much that way.

MIXING

Mixing is probably the least understood, most undervalued part of the baking process, because most people don't appreciate how many variables there are to mixing. It's not just a matter of getting all the ingredients combined; it's also about getting them to come together the right way.

Unless a recipe calls for ingredients to be hot or cold, it's best to go the Goldilocks route and have them just right, by which I mean at room temperature. This is especially true of butter and eggs, whose temperature can have a profound effect on how dough comes together.

Also, always be very careful not to overmix: in many recipes, the dry ingredients are the last to be added; as soon as they are incorporated, stop mixing or you risk ending up with a final product that's tighter, tougher, and more rubbery than you want it to be. The reason? Overmixing activates the protein in the flour and can also produce air bubbles.

Be sure to use the attachment called for in each recipe: the hook, paddle, and whip all produce different effects and are required for specific reasons. Generally speaking, the whip is used when you want to aerate ingredients—such as egg whites—as much as possible; a hook is called on to produce a kneading-like result (for example, with the babas on page 103); and a paddle is the default for just about everything else.

REDISCOVERING THE LOST ART OF ROLLING WITH A PIN

Walk into just about any bakery these days, and you'll see dough being flattened out by a sheeter, a powerful piece of motorized equipment that rolls dough—sometimes massive quantities of it—out into flat sheets. There's nothing wrong with using a sheeter; it's efficient and consistent. But when I was coming up, every baker I knew could achieve with a rolling pin what most young bakers need a sheeter to pull off today.

Home cooks don't have the luxury of using a sheeter, so you really have no choice but to become proficient with a rolling pin if you want to bake at a certain level, and I think that's a wonderful thing, a real link to the craftsmanship that used to define many great home bakers and my trade, and still does at Carlo's and some other tradition-bound bakeries. Rolling dough affects everything from how evenly it bakes to the texture of the final product to how it looks.

One of the keys to working with a pin is: Do not make the mistake of flour-

---

Scraping

We have a saying at Carlo's: Bakers scrape. By that we mean that whenever we mix something, we constantly stop the machine to scrape the sides and bottom of the bowl, to be sure that no dry or unmixed ingredients are eluding the hook, whip, or paddle. At home, when using a stand mixer, I recommend that you loosen the bowl so it drops down and you can get your spatula under the mixing attachment. Whenever you see instructions in this book to scrape, I mean to do this; it takes only a few extra seconds, and the result is worth it.

---

ing the pin. It looks good, but doesn't really help until deep into the process (see below). Instead, you should flour the work surface beneath the dough and flour the dough itself.

Generally speaking, when rolling with a straight pin—say, rolling out a pie crust—begin rolling up and down the center, then turn the dough sideways and roll over the center again. Then roll just right of center (toward the 1 or 2 o'clock position), then just left of center (toward the 10 or 11 o'clock position). Finally, roll the dough up on the pin, and unspool it over the pie pan.

When working with a ball-bearing pin, roll over the center of the dough heavily to really stretch it out. Then roll the sides down and out to even the dough's thickness. Roll the dough up on the pin, reflour your work surface, then unspool the dough so the side that was touching the work surface is now facing upward. Roll it, starting at the far end and pulling the pin toward you, then back out, first in the middle, then the sides. Continue like this, turning the dough over again and reflouring your work surface (and the pin, if the dough begins to pull or tear), until you achieve the desired thickness.

Getting the Most Out of Your Oven

I have lots of admiration for home bakers. Being in a professional bakery, I sometimes take for granted how hard it is to bake from home. At Carlo's Bake Shop, our ovens are works of art. They look primitive: huge, square boxes that are heated from the bottom. But the secret to their success is their rotating shelves that eliminate any hot spots; this is especially important with larger items like cakes, which are more affected by hot spots.

Your home oven might not be as impressive to look at as our monster ovens, but if you get to know it well, and learn its strengths and quirks, you two can make beautiful music together. Here are a few tips.

- *Keep it clean.* When was the last time you cleaned your oven? If you're like most home cooks, the answer is, "Um, well, I'm not really sure . . ." (This is especially unfortunate because I bet 99 percent of you have self-cleaning ovens that make the job a breeze.) Cooked-on food, especially those bits that look like chunks of charcoal fused to the wall or floor of the oven, will throw smoke, and that smoke can show up in the flavor of your baked goods. So be sure your oven is clean, and don't forget to scrub the racks as well; they sometimes catch food before it makes it to the oven floor, especially cheese and other sticky foods.

- *Seal it up.* An oven is like your home—if it is not properly insulated, hot air escapes. This probably won't affect your heating bill, but it will throw off your baking time. The cook times in this book assume a nice, steady temperature throughout the process. A well-sealed oven is one way to be sure that's the case. Another is to keep from opening the door during baking; use the oven light and visual cues to monitor doneness as long as possible without allowing heat to escape. When you do open the oven door, get it closed again as quickly as possible.
- *Be prepared.* Preheat the oven before you start baking so it's ready to receive whatever it is you're baking. Before you preheat, be sure the rack is placed where you want it (usually the center).
- *Don't overcrowd.* It's best to bake only one pan of cookies or pastries at a time. At the very least, you should bake on only one rack to ensure even cooking. Try to bake at a time when you can bake each tray on its own for optimum heat circulation.
- *Help your oven.* If you have a small oven, use trays and pans that are smaller than the oven's racks. Do not use pans that totally cover the oven rack, because this will prevent hot air from circulating freely. Because your oven has hot spots, when you're baking sheets of cookies or pastries it's a good idea to turn the pans around midway through the cooking time to ensure even cooking. Also, don't bake partially filled pans of cookies or pastries; the heat won't be distributed evenly and you'll be likely to wind up burning what you're baking. If you have a small batch, gather the pieces in the center of the pan.

Cookies

My baking education started with cookies. They taught me the fundamentals of my craft, and helped me develop muscle memory and intuition to last a lifetime.

But before I get into all that, let me sing the praises of cookies. Carlo's Bake Shop, like most Italian-American bakeries, has a counter section devoted to cookies, and it's the only section that's equally popular with adults and kids. That's because there are precious few new cookies in the world; most of the treats you see under that gleaming glass are exactly the same ones that moms and dads, grandmothers and grandfathers, ate when they were kids, too. The cookies might be something as simple as a black-and-white cookie or rugelach, but I love watching customers dig into them. Their faces say it all—kids are forming taste memories to last a lifetime; grown-ups are reliving their own memories with each bite.

My own memories of cookies date back to long before I ever tried to actually bake anything. When I was a child, my father would often return home from our family business, Carlo's Bake Shop, with a box of *tarelles* (vanilla cookies) or tea biscuits in hand. Dad was known around Hoboken as a cake master, but it was the cookies that mesmerized me. Most kids feel that way. Cakes are big, towering, intimidating: Before you can eat them, a grown-up has to slice them down to size for you.

But cookies are manageable—you can eat them in just one or two bites. And when I look back at my baking education, it's the same: Cookies were a way of taking in bite-size bits of information about basic skills and techniques, in a way that even a little kid could understand. It was by making cookies that I first learned how to mix dough properly, how to use a rolling pin, and how to start to develop the all-important Hand of the Bag.

The recipes in this chapter produce some of my favorite cookies, and it's a pretty varied bunch that reflects a number of cultures: *pignoli* (pine nut) cookies from Sicily, black-and-white cookies from New York City, Jewish rugelach, and all-American creations such as peanut butter cookies, to name just a few.

For home bakers, a good cookie recipe is a valuable thing. Most cookies can

be made quickly and stored for days, if not longer—so you can make them for guests and serve them right out of the oven or keep them on hand for unexpected company. They are also a good project for baking with kids who can do the simple tasks such as adding chocolate chips to dough. In addition to making cookies for family and friends, one of my favorite things to do with cookies is to give them as gifts. Think about giving cookies at the holidays or for a friend's birthday; there's nothing that shows your affection like baking something for someone yourself.

Cookies' simplicity is also the source of their power to teach us about baking. The more simple something is, the more important each part of it becomes. Most cookie recipes are made up of some combination of the same basic ingredients—butter, sugar, flour, eggs, and baking powder and/or baking soda—plus others that add flavor and texture. How those ingredients are mixed has everything to do with how the batter will behave when baked. You don't tend to see mixing discussed much outside professional bakeries, but in a place like Carlo's, we talk about it like it *is* rocket science. Every cookie requires its own style of mixing: Some need to be mixed quickly, some slowly, some for a long time, some not so much. (My own Achilles' heel as a kid was overwhipping egg whites; I'd let them go until they began to break down, their stiff peaks crumbling like an avalanche in the bowl.) The same is true of pastry and pie dough and cake batter: The difference between an Italian sponge cake batter and a chocolate chiffon batter is profound; being able to understand that begins by learning to understand the differences between the doughs for different cookies.

Cookies are also a good way to begin a baking education because the recipes are more forgiving than those for pastries or cakes. (They also multiply better, so you can double or triple them easily.) What's more, in professional bakeries,

Baking in Batches

Even if you have two or more pans, you will need to bake in batches for many of these recipes. Be sure to let the pans cool completely between batches. Putting raw dough on a warm or hot pan can cause the cookies to drop and cause the butter or shortening inside to melt prematurely. It's okay to let the dough just sit while the pans cool—and it's worth it so the cookies come out right.

Cooling Cookies

It's important to get cookies out of their hot pan and onto a rack as soon as possible after they come out of the oven. Test them with the edge of a spatula to see if they will lift up easily without breaking. As soon as they do, move them. If they are left on the pan too long and become stuck, don't use your spatula like a crowbar; instead, rewarm them briefly in the oven to loosen them up.

cookies are valuable commodities because many of them are convenient: Often, doughs and the finished cookies they produce can be frozen, so we can work them into the production schedule whenever we need to fit them in, and always have cookies on hand or just a few minutes of bake time away. Throughout this chapter, I'll point out when you can take advantage of this same convenience factor at home, so you always have cookies on tap.

Some cookies also teach you how to work with dough, rolling and molding it with your hands, and in some cases with a rolling pin—what we call "bench work" at Carlo's. And they teach the delicate balance between following a recipe and going with your gut in the kitchen. Think back to the first time you baked a chocolate chip cookie. I bet you overbaked it and ended up with something as hard as a manhole cover. That's because you didn't yet know that a chocolate chip cookie has to come out of the oven looking doughy, almost raw. But let it rest for an hour and it firms up to perfection, because the baking soda does its thing as the cookie cools down. We all need to learn the same lesson when it comes to

Storing Cookies

Do not put any cookies into a storage container until they have cooled completely. If you put them away warm, their heat will be trapped in the container and the steam will leave behind moisture that will cause them to spoil.

cookies—that we often have to take them out looking a little raw, trusting our baking experience to know that's the right thing to do.

The other, and most overlooked, thing that cookies can teach us is familiarity with our equipment and our ovens. By making cookies, I gained a real intimacy with our oven at Carlo's. This is even more important at home, because your home oven almost certainly has hot spots, and will not cook evenly like a professional oven. Making cookies let me learn that I like working with a broomstick handle for certain doughs (you'd buy a straight rolling pin to get the same effect) and a ball-bearing pin for others; and I learned which type of pastry bag I preferred for different jobs. But there's no one way of doing anything: You might have different preferences, and if they work for you, that's fine with me.

But you won't be able to learn any of that until you get into the kitchen and start baking. So, come on—let's make some cookies!

Butter Cookies

MAKES 48 COOKIES (24 REGULAR AND 24 CHOCOLATE)

These are softer than the butter cookies that come stacked in doilies and sold in round aluminum tins. They're also a little chewier, thanks to the almond paste in the dough. But what they have in common with their popular, mass-produced cousins is that they can be formed into a variety of shapes.

This is one of the first recipes my father taught me to make, so I wanted it to be the first one I share with you. I still remember him showing me how to mix the dough, starting by creaming together the almond paste and butter (this is a crucial step; see "Creaming," opposite), then adding the wet ingredients, and then the flour, mixing and scraping to break up any stubborn lumps. I still hear him coaching me when I make these. "It's all about the *method*," he'd say, explaining that overmixing would cause the cookies to lose their shape and fall like a puddle when baked or be too fragile. He could pull eight hot pans full of these cookies out of the oven so fast the temperature barely dropped, then get the next pans in and on their way. When I tried to match his speed the first time I baked these, removing two trays at once, I scorched my forearm and dropped the pans.

"That's okay, Buddy," he told me. "When you use a knife for the first time you cut yourself; when you do this, you get burned."

Note: This recipe makes 24 plain cookies and 24 chocolate. You can make them all chocolate by doubling the amount of cocoa, or all plain by leaving it out.

2 cups (4 sticks) unsalted butter
1 cup sugar
¾ cup almond paste
4 extra-large egg whites
3½ cups cake flour (no substitutions)
1 tablespoon unsweetened Dutch-process cocoa powder

1. Position a rack in the center of the oven and preheat to 350°F.
2. Cream the butter, sugar, and almond paste in the bowl of a mixer fitted with the paddle attachment. (You can use a hand mixer if you allow the butter to soften at room temperature before beginning.) Starting on low speed, and increasing to medium after 2 minutes, paddle the ingredients until uniformly smooth with a mashed potato consistency, about 5 minutes.
3. Lower the mixer speed to low and pour in about one quarter of the egg whites. Paddle for 1 minute, then stop and scrape with a rubber spatula. Paddle on low speed and add another quarter of the egg whites, again paddling for 1 minute, then stop to scrape again. Repeat until all egg whites have been added, paddling for 1 minute extra at the end to ensure the dough is smooth.
4. Add the flour and paddle just until it is absorbed into the dough and the dough is smooth again. (The dough may be wrapped in plastic wrap and refrigerated for up to 1 week, or frozen for up to 1 month; let it come to room temperature before proceeding with the recipe.)
5. Transfer half the dough to a pastry bag fitted with a #7 star tip.
6. Working on one or two nonstick cookie sheets, pipe the dough into 2½-inch circles (see "Practice Makes Perfect: Piping with Steady Pressure," page 44), leaving about 1½ inches between circles, and create four staggered rows of three circles each.
7. Bake the cookies in batches for about 12 minutes or until the bottoms are tinged golden-brown (lift very gently with a spatula to check underneath if necessary) and the star-tip ridges have dropped into a shallow, wavy pat-

Creaming

Creaming butter and another ingredient such as almond paste is often the first step in mixing cookie dough and it should not be taken for granted. This base needs to be mixed enough that it aerates, which will set the stage for the cookies to achieve the proper body and texture and help keep them from crumbling too easily. This step often includes a granular ingredient such as sugar that acts almost like sandpaper, smoothing out lumps as early in the recipe as possible.

tern. Remove the cookie sheets from the oven. As soon as the cookies can be moved, use a spatula to transfer them to a rack and let them cool. (Be sure to let the pans cool completely before piping the chocolate cookies on to them.)

8. Meanwhile, add the cocoa power to the remaining dough and paddle just until blended. Squeeze out any remaining plain dough from the pastry bag, then spoon the cocoa dough into the bag. Repeat steps 6 and 7 with the cocoa dough.

The cookies may be stored in an airtight container at room temperature for up to 2 weeks.

Practice Makes Perfect: Piping with Steady Pressure

These cookies call for piping with steady pressure, which will begin training your muscle memory for making cake borders, especially loop borders (see page 174). You can vary the shapes of these cookies, and give yourself practice with other piping techniques; for example, piping straight cookies (about 2 inches long) is a perfect way to work on squeeze-and-pull piping (see page 153).

By the way, here's a tip: Piping consistent circles of any size is harder than it seems. This recipe doesn't call for parchment paper, but until you develop the muscle memory to do this, trace circles on parchment paper in pencil using the mouth of a glass or a cookie cutter as your guide. Turn the paper over so the pencil is on the underside (that is, not touching the dough), line your cookie sheet with it, and use it to trace circles as you pipe. Do this until you find it's no longer necessary, which might be sooner than you think!

Double Chocolate Chip Cookies

There is nothing subtle about these cookies, which combine a rich, chewy, black-as-night cookie with chocolate chips. You know that popular cake, Death by Chocolate? Well, this is Death by Chocolate that you can fit in the palm of your hand. But don't be fooled by its size; it packs a huge, crowd-pleasing punch of texture and flavor.

The story behind this cookie illustrates the way new recipes come to be in a bake shop. To create it, I began with my dad's chocolate chip cookie recipe. The first order of business was to figure out how to make a chocolate cookie, which you achieve by replacing some of the flour with cocoa. But it's not a simple one-to-one ratio and the only way to solve the problem is by trial and error. I spent hours in the back of the bakery making batch after batch of this, adjusting the quantities of flour to cocoa until I got it just right.

Finally, I came up with this recipe, which I think is one of our very best, and to really put it over the top, I decided to make it with just dark semisweet chocolate chips, rather than a combination of dark and less-rich milk chocolate, which gets lost in the midst of all these strong flavors. It's not often I think I've hit upon perfection—most things can be improved, even if you can't immediately see how to do it—but this, to me, is a perfect cookie. I hope you enjoy it.

1 cup (2 sticks) unsalted butter
1 cup granulated sugar
½ cup light brown sugar
⅓ cup unsweetened Dutch-process cocoa powder
1 extra-large egg
1 teaspoon pure vanilla extract
2 tablespoons whole milk
1¾ cups all-purpose flour
¼ teaspoon baking powder
1 cup semisweet chocolate chips

1. Position a rack in the center of the oven and preheat to 325°F.
2. Put the butter, sugar, and brown sugar in the bowl of a stand mixer fitted with the paddle attachment. (You can use a hand mixer if you allow the butter to soften at room temperature before beginning.) Cream on low speed until the mixture is uniformly blended, with no pieces of butter remaining, 2 to 3 minutes.
3. Add the cocoa, egg, and vanilla. Mix on low for 1 to 2 minutes, then stop and scrape with a rubber spatula. Mix on low speed until the mixture resembles chocolate frosting, 2 to 3 minutes. Stop and scrape, then add the milk and paddle for 30 seconds to blend it in.
4. Put the flour and baking powder in a separate mixing bowl and stir together with a fork or whisk. Add to the mixer bowl and paddle on low speed until well mixed, about 1 minute. Scrape and mix for another minute on low speed. With the mixer running on low speed, add the chocolate chips and mix just until evenly distributed, about 1 minute. (The dough can be wrapped in plastic wrap and refrigerated for up to 1 week or frozen for up to 2 months. Let come to room temperature before proceeding with the recipe.)
5. When ready to bake the cookies, break the dough into small pieces and roll between the palms of your hands to form 24 meatball-size balls. Place on two nonstick cookie sheets, about 2 inches apart.
6. Bake until the cookies are flat and hot, 13 to 15 minutes. The cookies will

---

Sizing Up Your Cookies

When bakers boast of being able to roll or bag portions of dough out uniformly, like a machine, it's much more than a point of pride. All the cookies in a batch should be the same size or they will not cook evenly, and the same is true of pastries. This recipe is a good one for starting to develop that skill because you break the dough up by hand, so if one cookie looks too small or large, you can add to or take away from it. Just be careful not to overwork it as you make adjustments. If you happen to end up with fewer cookies than the indicated yield, that means you have made them too big and the cooking time will probably be slightly longer than indicated; if you end up with too many cookies, you made them too small and the cooking time will probably be shorter.

look underdone, but will gently finish baking after you remove them from the oven. Do not leave in the oven for more than 15 minutes, no matter what. Remove the cookie sheets from the oven. As soon as the cookies can be moved, use a spatula to transfer them to a rack and let them cool.

The cookies can be kept in an airtight container at room temperature for up to 3 days. You can continue to eat them for up to 1 week, but they will harden after 3 days. If you want, you can soften them by warming in the microwave for 5 to 10 seconds on the "high" setting.

Peanut Butter Cookies

MAKES 30 TO 36 COOKIES

This chewy-gooey cookie was devised by my brother-in-law, Joey Faugno, who heads up the baking department at Carlo's, and it brilliantly re-creates the flavor profile of a peanut butter cup—that irresistible combination of peanut butter and chocolate—by adapting the bakery's recipe for chocolate chip cookies, taking out some of the liquid, and including a combination of peanut butter chips and milk chocolate chips, which get along better than the dark chocolate we use in the original. (Thanks to Joey's fondness for "extra chippy" cookies, these have more chips per square inch than our chocolate chip cookies.)

When baking these, it's crucial to keep carryover cooking (the way foods continue to cook by their own heat after they are removed from the oven) in mind; don't let them spend too much time in the oven. As with a great chocolate chip cookie, you want them to be cooked through but soft and pliable. Use a spatula to peek underneath: As soon as the bottom is lightly browned, get them out.

At Carlo's, we store our peanut butter in the basement, where it can get see-your-own-breath cold in the wintertime, causing the peanut butter to separate and producing a layer of oil on top. So we add an extra step to the recipe, mixing

Making the Cut

It's tempting to freeze dough in cylinders because we've all seen that slice-your-own ready-made dough in the supermarket. But it's better to freeze raw cookies after cutting them because it will speed the thawing process when you're ready to bake. After cutting them, dust them with flour to keep them from sticking, put them in a freezer bag, and freeze them. When ready to bake, let thaw completely, roll, press, and bake as described in the recipe.

the peanut butter in the mixer to reincorporate the oil before adding the other ingredients. If you refrigerate your peanut butter or have a house as cold as our basement, be sure to do the same.

You can make these with all peanut butter chips, all chocolate chips, or—to really drive home the peanut butter flavor—an addition of chopped, unsalted peanuts.

¾ cup creamy peanut butter
¼ cup vegetable shortening (such as Crisco)
¼ cup tightly packed light brown sugar
1 extra-large egg
One 14-ounce can sweetened condensed milk
1 teaspoon pure vanilla extract
1½ cups all-purpose flour, plus more for flouring your work surface
2 teaspoons baking powder
½ cup milk chocolate chips
½ cup peanut butter chips
½ cup unsalted peanuts, chopped (optional)

1. Position a rack in the center of the oven and preheat to 325°F.
2. Put the peanut butter, shortening, and sugar in the bowl of a stand mixer fitted with the paddle attachment. (You can use a hand mixer if you let the peanut butter soften at room temperature before beginning.) Cream together at low speed to ensure there are no lumps. Add the egg and paddle at medium speed until the ingredients are blended together, about 1 minute. Stop and scrape with a rubber spatula.
3. Add the condensed milk and vanilla extract. Paddle on low speed for 1 minute, stop and scrape, then continue to mix until the mixture is smooth and shiny, about another 30 seconds. Turn off the mixer.

Rolling by Hand

Handling the cookie dough here is a good way to start to develop your feeling for working with fondant (see page 199).

---

4. Put the flour and baking powder in a small bowl and stir together with a fork or whisk. Add to the mixer bowl. Mix on low speed for about 1 minute. Stop and scrape. Continue to mix on low speed for another minute. Then, with the motor running, sprinkle in the chocolate and peanut butter chips. If you're adding the chopped peanuts, add them at this point. Keep mixing just until the chips are evenly distributed, 30 seconds to 1 minute. (The dough can be wrapped in plastic wrap and refrigerated for up to 1 week or frozen for up to 2 months. Let it come to room temperature before proceeding with the recipe.)

5. Line two cookie sheets with parchment paper, using nonstick spray or a dab of butter in each corner to glue the paper in place. (If you have more than two cookie sheets, line a third sheet to speed up the process of baking in batches.)

6. Flour a work surface and turn the dough out onto the surface. Divide the dough in half. Roll one half out into a cylinder 20 inches long and 1 inch in diameter. Use a knife to cut the dough crosswise into 1-inch segments. (You should have 15 to 18 segments.) Quickly roll each segment into a ball and press down with the palm of your hand until the dough is squeezed down to ½ inch high. (You don't want to take too much time rolling each one or your hands will warm up the dough too much.) Arrange the discs on the pans, about 12 per pan, about 1 inch from the edge and 2 inches apart.

7. Repeat with the remaining dough.

8. Bake the cookies in batches until golden-brown on top and brown at the edges, about 8 minutes. (If they crack a little bit on top, that's all right.) The

Baking Soda Versus Baking Powder

Have you ever wondered why some recipes call for baking soda, some for baking powder, and some for a combination? Baking powder causes batters to rise (the best example is pancakes—they'd be really flat without that smidgen of baking powder in the recipe), while baking soda causes it to drop and spread. It's important to carefully measure all ingredients, but especially something that has such a scientific effect, so be sure to level off the soda in your measuring spoon before adding it to the bowl.

cookies will still be soft, but the carryover heat will finish cooking them. Remove the cookie sheets from the oven. As soon as the cookies can be moved, after about 10 minutes, use a spatula to transfer them to a rack and let them cool.

These cookies are best enjoyed as soon as they have cooled enough to handle and eat, but will keep for up to 2 days in an airtight container at room temperature.

Chocolate Brownie Clusters

MAKES 18 CLUSTERS

In a bakery like Carlo's, everybody contributes some recipes at some time or another. These cookies—which replicate the flavors and textures of a brownie in a meringue-like cookie that's miraculously crisp on the outside and gooey in the middle—were the invention of the late, great baker Sal Picinich (who passed away while I was writing this book) and they're pretty ingenious.

What impresses me about these cookies is the complex, deeply satisfying result achieved with just a handful of ingredients: egg whites, sugar, cocoa, and nuts. The batter looks like an unholy, goopy-gooey mess. When you make these, you might even think you did something wrong—how could it transform into something appetizing? Your doubt might even be increased by the fact that these can only be spooned onto your baking sheet; the dough is too sticky for a pastry bag and too messy to work with by hand.

But trust me: Once these get into the oven, something magical happens and these ugly ducklings turn into perfect little swans—and everybody will love the way they mimic the flavor and texture of brownies. It's a cookie to die for.

3 extra-large egg whites
½ teaspoon freshly squeezed lemon juice
1½ cups powdered (10X) sugar
¼ cup unsweetened Dutch-process cocoa powder
1½ cups unsalted raw walnut halves

1. Position a rack in the center of the oven and preheat to 325°F.
2. Put the egg whites and lemon juice in the bowl of a stand mixer fitted with the whip attachment. (Be sure the bowl is immaculately clean; see "Egg Whites," page 56.) Whip on low speed for 2 minutes, then on maximum speed until stiff peaks form, about 5 minutes.
3. Sift the sugar and cocoa powder into the bowl together, then fold into the

batter with a rubber spatula until the batter is smooth and shiny. Fold in the walnuts, until they are well coated with the batter.

4. Line two cookie sheets with parchment paper, using nonstick spray or a dab of butter in each corner to glue the paper in place. Drop heaping tablespoons of dough ½ inch apart, being sure to include about the same number of walnuts (3 or 4) in each one.

5. Bake until the outside has crisped and the bottom starts to pull away from the parchment paper, 15 to 20 minutes.

6. Remove the cookie sheet from the oven. As soon as the clusters can be moved, use a spatula to transfer them to a rack and let them cool.

Enjoy the cookies right away, or store when completely cool in an airtight container at room temperature for up to 1 week.

Sifting

I sift ingredients for two reasons: (1) To be sure dry ingredients aren't too compacted; sifting helps ensure a lighter result in the baked good being made. (2) To better combine two or more dry ingredients that will be added to a recipe at the same time. This is especially important when you are using leavening agents such as baking powder and baking soda—you want those strong-acting ingredients to be as evenly distributed as possible to ensure an even result across the entire baked good. (All of that said, in some cookie recipes I don't call for sifting because the dough gets mixed enough that the ingredients can't help being evenly distributed.)

Egg Whites

Egg whites are one of the most important ingredients in baking. More than almost any other ingredient, they can determine the density of everything from a cookie to a cake. If you want to understand the effect cooks are looking for in the finished product, note how they tell you to whip your whites: stiff peaks usually means the desired effect is a full-bodied finished product.

In this recipe, the whites should be whipped until they are stiff, and that is what allows the batter to expand the way it does.

However you whip them, there are a few important things to remember about working with egg whites:

First of all, your bowl must be immaculately clean. Wipe it down with distilled white vinegar to get rid of all traces of grease and oil; fat will prevent the whites from stiffening.

When you are whipping egg whites, the addition of an acid (this recipe uses lemon juice; in some other recipes, cream of tartar has the same effect) helps produce maximum peaks. Believe it or not, using eggs that are older (but not past their "best by" date) also helps; the proteins are more relaxed, so they froth up better. And for the best results, start whipping whites at room temperature, on low speed. Keep your mixer on low for 2 minutes, then increase the speed. Be sure to use the whites as soon as possible after whipping them; they will begin to drop before too long.

Pignoli Cookies
Pine Nut Cookies

MAKES ABOUT 48 COOKIES

Pine nuts are a real delicacy that most of us here in America are used to seeing in savory cooking—they're one of the key ingredients in pesto and are often tossed into pastas and other Italian staples to add earthy crunch.

I discovered another use for pine nuts on a trip to Sicily years ago: using them in a cookie that treats them as nuts, the same way we'd use almonds or walnuts here. These cookies would be delicious even without the pine nuts— almond paste, cinnamon, and honey lend an addictively aromatic quality and chewy texture—but the nuts really put these over the top and make them something truly special.

Note that the raw cookies need to rest overnight before baking; otherwise they won't hold their shape and will drop when baked, a lesson that more than a few impatient young bakers have learned the hard way at Carlo's.

> 2½ cups tightly packed almond paste (1 pound 9 ounces)
> 1¼ cups granulated sugar
> ½ cup powdered (10X) sugar
> 1 heaping teaspoon ground cinnamon
> 1 tablespoon honey, preferably clover
> 1 teaspoon pure vanilla extract
> 5 extra-large egg whites
> 5 cups pine nuts (about 1½ pounds)

1. Put the almond paste, granulated sugar, powdered sugar, cinnamon, honey, and vanilla in the bowl of a stand mixer fitted with the paddle attachment. (You can also use a hand mixer.) Paddle at low-medium speed until the mixture is smooth with no lumps remaining, about 1 minute.

2. With the motor running, add the egg whites in three installments and paddle until absorbed, 30 seconds to 1 minute per addition.
3. Cut five 12-inch squares of parchment paper. Arrange a square of parchment paper on a work surface. Put the dough in a pastry bag fitted with a #6 plain tip and pipe the dough out into circles, 2 inches in diameter and about 1½ inches high, leaving about 2 inches between circles. Repeat on four remaining pieces of parchment.
4. Spread the pine nuts out on a cookie sheet in a single layer. Take one of the cookie dough–covered parchment sheets in two hands and slowly invert it over the nuts. Press down so that nuts adhere to the dough and remove, very gently shaking the parchment to loosen any extra nuts. Set the nut-coated dough aside. Shake the cookie sheet to redistribute the pine nuts, and repeat with the remaining dough-covered sheets until all cookies are coated with pine nuts. Save any unused nuts for another use.
5. Leave the prepared cookies out uncovered at room temperature overnight or for 8 hours to dry.
6. When ready to bake the cookies, position a rack in the center of the oven and preheat to 350°F.
7. Set one of the parchment sheets on a baking tray and bake until the cookies are nicely golden, about 20 minutes. Remove the tray from the oven, carefully transfer the parchment to a heatproof surface to let the cookies cool, and bake the next sheet on the tray. Repeat

Pine Nuts

I recommend that you buy Spanish or Portuguese pine nuts, because they have the best flavor. They are expensive, but you will not use all of them in this recipe. The 5 cups called for will coat the cookies when you press them into the nuts. Alternatively, you could buy just 2½ cups of nuts (1¼ pounds) and press them into the cookies by hand, but that would be very time-consuming.

until all cookies are baked, and let cool for approximately 20 minutes before serving.

The cookies can be held in an airtight container at room temperature for up to 1 week, or wrapped in plastic and frozen for up to 1 month. Let come to room temperature before serving.

What's in a Name?

Do *not* buy marzipan for this recipe; it's not the same as almond paste—marzipan is sweeter!

Seven-Layer Cookies

MAKES 32 COOKIES

You might know these cookies by their other names, tri-color cookies or rainbow cookies. They are one of the most popular treats sold in Italian-American bakeries—pink, green, chocolate, and white layers with raspberry jam spread between them, cut into little squares or rectangles.

From a baking standpoint, the secret of these cookies is that each layer is made with the same base, so they might be easier to make than you ever imagined. You divide the batter into five equal batches, leaving two white, coloring one pink, coloring another one green, and flavoring the last with cocoa, turning it dark brown. Then you spread each dough out in a pan, bake it, and assemble the cookie. My personal twist is to sometimes layer semisweet chocolate or the chocolate-hazelnut spread, Nutella, between the different cakes rather than jam.

Be especially careful not to overbake the individual layers; because they are so thin and delicate, they can disintegrate if they spend too much time in the oven.

You can layer the colors in whatever order you like, but according to Carlo's Bake Shop tradition, we always put the chocolate in the middle, so that's how I make them here.

Note that you will need five 8-inch-square disposable aluminum baking pans. Also note that you *must* weigh down the cookies as indicated in the recipe before coating them with chocolate and cutting them. A few years back, on a particularly busy day, we didn't have room for freshly baked and assembled seven-layer cookies upstairs, so I instructed an intern to take the batch to the basement and put a hundred-pound sack of sugar on top of them overnight. He thought we were pulling his leg, so he took them downstairs, but skipped the sugar-sack step. The next day, after coating them in chocolate, we sliced the cookies . . . and the stack fell apart like a house of cards. Like I always say, every step matters in baking!

1½ cups (3 sticks) unsalted butter, plus more for greasing the pans
2 cups powdered (10X) sugar
¼ teaspoon pure vanilla extract
¼ cup freshly squeezed lemon juice
7 extra-large eggs
2 cups all-purpose flour
¼ teaspoon pink food-coloring gel
¼ teaspoon green food-coloring gel
1 teaspoon unsweetened Dutch-process cocoa powder
4 heaping tablespoons raspberry jam
2 cups semisweet chocolate chips or coarsely chopped semisweet chocolate
    (12 ounces)

1. Position a rack in the center of the oven, and preheat to 350°F.
2. Grease each of the aluminum pans with butter and line them with parchment paper, pressing the paper down into the pan so it is well sealed.
3. In the bowl of a stand mixer fitted with the paddle attachment, cream the butter, sugar, vanilla, and lemon juice at low speed, gradually increasing to medium. Add the eggs (two at a time, one in the last batch) and paddle for about 1 minute, stopping to scrape after every batch. After all eggs have been added, add the flour and paddle until it is fully absorbed, without any lumps, 1 to 2 more minutes.
4. Spread about ¾ cup of the batter into each of two pans, ⅛ to ¼ inch deep, and smooth with a rubber spatula. This will make your white cake.
5. Transfer another ¾ cup of the batter from the mixer into a bowl and add the pink gel. Stir in with a rubber spatula until the mixture is uniformly pink. Spread the mixture into one of the baking pans, ⅛ to ¼ inch deep, and smooth with a rubber spatula. This will make your pink cake.
6. Transfer another ¾ cup of the batter from the mixer into another bowl and add the green gel. Stir in with a rubber spatula until the mixture is uniformly green. Spread the mixture into one of the baking pans, ⅛ to ¼ inch deep, and smooth with a rubber spatula. This will make your green cake.
7. Add the cocoa powder to the remaining batter in the mixer. Stir in with a rubber spatula until the mixture is uniformly brown. Spread the mixture into the last baking pan, ⅛ to ¼ inch deep, and smooth with a rubber spatula. This will make your chocolate cake.
8. Bake the cakes on the center rack of the oven; two pans in each of the first two batches, and one pan at the end. Bake until the cakes are just set and

barely golden (if they overbake, they will fall apart when you try to work with them), about 15 minutes.

9. Remove the trays from the oven and let the cakes cool completely in the pans.

10. Unmold one white layer and turn it over so the parchment paper is on its downward-facing side. Spread 1 heaping tablespoon of raspberry jam over the layer, as thinly and uniformly as possible, using an offset spatula. Invert the pink layer over it and pull the parchment off. Top with another heap-

---

Treat Your Chocolate Right

I'll never forget the way the old-timers at Carlo's used to leave a pot of chocolate boiling away for eternity on the stovetop. You'd never know that this wasn't really the way to treat chocolate, which should be warmed over very low heat. For all of our devotion to the time-honored ways of doing things, this was one tradition that we stopped—and we saved good money and made even better baked goods as a result.

To melt chocolate, coarsely chop it and put it in a double boiler set over *simmering* (not boiling) water. (To skip the chopping step, you can begin with chocolate chips.) Stir it with a rubber spatula until it's uniformly melted, and check the water periodically to be sure it isn't bubbling too aggressively.

Here's an old trick for monitoring the water without lifting the top pot off the boiler: put a coin in the bottom pot; you'll hear it tapping against the metal as the water simmers. If the tapping is too fast, the water is bubbling too aggressively. It it's too slow, you can turn the heat up a little. If it stops tapping, you have probably run out of water and you need to add more. Be very careful not to let any water find its way into the pot with the chocolate; it will cause the chocolate to seize up. (For the same reason, do not cover chocolate as it melts; the condensation that forms on the inside of the cover will drip into the chocolate. Game over!)

You can also melt chocolate in a microwave. Put the chocolate in a microwave-safe bowl and microwave it for 30 seconds. Remove the bowl from the microwave and give the chocolate a stir with a rubber spatula. If it is not warm and soft enough, heat for another 30 seconds. Continue to repeat and stir until the chocolate is nicely molten.

---

ing tablespoon of jam, again spreading it out as thinly as possible with the spatula. Continue to build the layers in this way, unmolding cake layers, removing the parchment, and topping each layer with a heaping tablespoon of jam and spreading it out, adding the chocolate, green, and second white layer, in that order. (Leave the parchment paper on the outside of the white layer, so the top and bottom of the stack are protected by parchment.)

11. Press the cookies: Put the cookies on a pan and top with another pan. Weight the top pan with heavy cans (such as cans of tomatoes) and refrigerate for at least 1 hour, or overnight.

12. When ready to proceed, melt the chocolate in the top of a double boiler over simmering water. (For more, see "Treat Your Chocolate Right," opposite.) Remove the parchment paper from the white layers. Use an offset spatula to spread the chocolate over the top of the stack. Let it harden, about 5 minutes. (To quicken hardening, you can put the tray back in the refrigerator.) Flip the stack over and spread chocolate over the new top. Let harden. Refrigerate briefly to firm up the cookies and facilitate slicing.

13. Cut the cookies: Trim all four open sides of the stack with a serrated knife to square them. Cut four 2-inch-wide strips out of the stack, then cut the strips crosswise into 1-inch pieces.

The cookies may be kept in an airtight container at room temperature for up to 1 week, or frozen for up to 3 weeks; let thaw to room temperature before serving.

Chill!

Whenever you need to trim or cut a cakey cookie, it's very helpful to refrigerate it briefly to firm it up and facilitate nice, even slices. As you can see on page 170, freezing cakes is a step I highly recommend for the same reason.

Tarelles

Vanilla Cookies

MAKES ABOUT 40 COOKIES

This basic cookie—one of the first ones I ever learned to make—is a wonderful one for gauging where you are in your early development as a baker. Because it's such a no-frills affair, there's nowhere to hide; its success depends entirely on proper mixing and baking.

When I was a kid, my father taught me to use both hands at the same time to roll these out, so I was able to make more of them, faster, than anybody else in the kitchen. This memory comes up for me often because these also happen to be my son Buddy Jr.'s favorite cookies to roll at the bakery on the weekends, and the fact that he's able to do such a great job with them at such a young age shows me that he's clearly got the same gifted hands that I have—and that my Dad had before me.

1¼ cups sugar
2 extra-large eggs
1 teaspoon pure vanilla extract
1¼ cups vegetable shortening
½ cup whole milk
2¼ cups all-purpose flour, plus more for flouring your work surface
2¼ cups pastry flour, or additional all-purpose flour
2 teaspoons baking powder

1. Position a rack in the center of the oven and preheat to 350°F.
2. Put the sugar, eggs, and vanilla in the bowl of a stand mixer fitted with the paddle attachment and paddle on low-medium speed until combined, approximately 2 minutes. With the motor running, add the shortening and paddle for 30 seconds. Pour in the milk and paddle until it's thoroughly absorbed into the mixture, approximately 2 minutes.

3. Stop the motor and add the flours and baking powder. Paddle on medium-high speed until it comes together into a smooth ball of dough and pulls away from the sides of the bowl, 3 to 5 minutes, then scrape down the bowl and paddle with a rubber spatula.

4. Lightly flour a work surface. Transfer the dough to the surface, and separate it into 2 equal pieces. Roll 1 piece into a rope about 1 inch in diameter and 30 inches long. Cut the dough into about twenty 1½-inch pieces. Roll each piece into a rope about 5 inches long and ½ inch in diameter, and bend to make a ring, pressing the ends together until they stick. (For a nice visual flourish, give these a twist effect; see "Making Twisty *Tarelles,*" opposite.) Put as many as possible on a nonstick cookie sheet about 1 inch apart.

5. Bake until golden brown on the bottom (check by gently lifting an edge with a spatula), approximately 15 minutes. Meanwhile, roll out the remaining piece of dough and form about another 20 cookies.

6. When the first batch is done, remove the cookie sheet from the oven, and as soon as the cookies can be moved, use a spatula to transfer them to a rack and let them cool. Once the cookie sheet has cooled, arrange another batch of cookies on the sheet, and repeat.

7. Continue to repeat until all the cookies have been baked and cooled, approximately 20 minutes after the last batch has come out of the oven. (If you have more than one cookie sheet, you can alternate, always having one sheet ready to go.)

The cookies will keep in an airtight container at room temperature for at least 1 week.

BUDDY VALASTRO

Making Twisty *Tarelles*

To make twisty *tarelles,* in step 4, roll the dough out into 10-inch lengths, fold each length in half, and roll against your work surface to cause it to spiral. Bend into a circle and pinch at the ends to keep it from coming apart.

Rugelach

MAKES 60 RUGELACH

Whenever my father hired a new baker, he would ask him if he had anything new he wanted to add to our repertoire. Having been a hired hand himself for a number of years, my father knew that most of the other bakers out there had a great recipe or two in their back pocket. When we hired Jimmy Lee, he offered up his version of the Jewish-American classic rugelach, which he had picked up, of all places, in a Greek diner where he used to work.

On slower days, when there was extra time, Jimmy taught me how to make rugelach. Not only was it a chance to take my rolling skills up a notch (see "Practice Makes Perfect: Rolling," page 74), but the dough was a thing of insane, addictive beauty: cream cheese, butter, sugar, flour—I must have eaten pounds of raw dough over the years. It's that delicious, and after it's baked . . . well, you'll see.

But you have not truly had rugelach until you've eaten them right out of the oven (let them sit for about 10 minutes to cool slightly). The dough is still warm, the flavors melt together, and each bite is a taste of heaven on earth.

1¼ cups (2½ sticks) unsalted butter
¾ cup powdered (10X) sugar
⅓ cup (⅔ stick) margarine
One 8-ounce package Philadelphia cream cheese
1¼ cups cake flour (no substitutions)
1¼ cups all-purpose flour, plus more for flouring your work surface
1 cup bake-proof raspberry jam (you can use regular jam if you spread it
    super thin; see "No Bake-Proof Jam?," page 73)
½ cup granulated sugar
½ teaspoon ground cinnamon
1 cup crushed, unsalted walnuts (4 ounces)
1 cup raisins
½ cup (1 stick) unsalted butter, melted

1. Put 1¼ cups butter, the powdered sugar, and the margarine in the bowl of a stand mixer fitted with the paddle attachment and cream together for 2 or 3 minutes, starting on slow and gradually increasing the speed to medium. (You can use a hand mixer if you allow the butter and margarine to soften at room temperature before beginning.) Break up the cream cheese and with the motor running on medium speed, add it to the mixture in pieces. Paddle for 2 to 3 minutes, then stop and scrape. Paddle until all ingredients are well blended, about 3 minutes more. Add the cake flour and all-purpose flour and mix on low for 1 to 2 minutes. Be careful not to overmix; stop as soon as the fats are homogenized and the dough is smooth, with no lumps.

2. Transfer the dough to a 1-gallon storage bag and flatten it out by hand to preshape it and give yourself a head start with rolling it out as thin as possible. (You can also wrap it in plastic wrap and flatten it out by hand.) Refrigerate overnight or up to 1 week.

3. When ready to proceed, let the dough come to room temperature, at least 1 to 1½ hours.

4. Position a rack in the center of the oven, and preheat to 350°F.

5. Generously flour a work surface. Unwrap the dough and set it on the surface. Flatten and shape it by hand into a 15 by 12-inch rectangle, then use a rolling pin (I prefer a ball-bearing pin for this), to roll it out to a 24 by 18-inch rectangle, about ⅛ inch thick. Use a bench brush to brush off any excess flour from on top of the dough.

6. Top the dough with the jam and spread it out thinly and evenly with a plastic scraper or the back edge of your knife.

7. In a small bowl, stir together the sugar and cinnamon. Scatter the nuts and raisins over the dough, then dust with half the cinnamon sugar. Lightly roll

---

Melting Butter

The most fail-safe way to melt butter is to do it in a pan over very low heat. You can also melt it in a microwave, but be careful: If it gets too hot, the water content can explode (that's the "popping" sound you heard if you ever overnuked your butter). Put the butter in a wide, shallow dish and cover it with plastic wrap to save yourself a mess in case that happens.

over the top with a rolling pin just to press the nuts and raisins into the dough.

8. Cut the dough lengthwise into four 6-inch strips, ideally with a pizza cutter. Cut the strips crosswise into three 6-inch pieces. You should have 12 pieces.

9. Roll up each piece tautly into a pinwheel about 1 inch in diameter, ending with the seam on the bottom.

10. Group the rolls into threes and use a pastry brush to paint the tops with melted butter. Quickly sprinkle some of the cinnamon sugar over the top, and repeat these steps with each group of three, until you have coated all the rugelach with butter and cinnamon sugar.

11. Flour your scraper or knife and cut each trio into 1½-inch pieces. You should have 60 pieces.

12. Line two cookie sheets with parchment paper, using nonstick spray or a dab of butter in each corner to glue the paper in place. Arrange the rolls, seam-side down, on the sheets, leaving ½ inch between them.

13. Bake in batches until the rugelach are browned on the bottom (note that these will not be very brown on top), 18 to 22 minutes. Remove the cookie sheet from the oven. As soon as the cookies can be moved, use a spatula to transfer them to a rack and let them cool.

Eat the rugelach as soon as they are cool enough to handle, or let cool completely, then store in an airtight container at room temperature for up to 1 week. They can also be frozen for up to 2 weeks; let come to room temperature before serving.

Variation: These are also delicious with apricot jam.

No Bake-Proof Jam?

Bake-proof jam can be hard to find if you don't have access to a foodservice purveyor like the ones who supply Carlo's. It's fine to use jam or preserves if you spread them very thin, but stay away from jelly, which is too unstable and will leak when baked.

Practice Makes Perfect: Rolling

Because the dough is relatively soft and pliable, this recipe offers a forgiving way to improve your skills with a rolling pin. As with so much in baking, you can learn only so much by being told: The real skills develop through practice, by developing muscle memory and an eye for accuracy.

Linzer Tart Cookies

MAKES 15 COOKIES

Linzer tart cookies look complicated—the two layers of cookie, the little hole in the center through which the raspberry jam shines through—but the truth is that they're made with a simple shortbread dough that forms both the top and the bottom layer. Usually flavor is all-important, but you really do eat this one with your eyes first. It's crucial to do good, clean work with the cookie mold and to bake the cookie just enough to set it without browning it.

Another detail that's also important: make sure you powder the tops before you put them on top of the jam-covered base; otherwise, it's too hard to keep the sugar from landing on the jam. It might not look that hard to do, but believe me, it is. When I was a teenage baker, I thought I was good enough to powder the cookies after adding the tops. For all the ability I showed at that age, I failed miserably at that shortcut, landing half the sugar on the jam that showed through in the center and having to donate the entire batch to the garbage. (You don't have to trash your cookies over a little sugar in the jam, of course, but Carlo's doesn't sell cookies that have this defect.) Ever since, and to this day, I make these the proper way, which—after all—doesn't take any more time than the wrong way.

1¾ cups vegetable shortening (such as Crisco)
½ cup granulated sugar
½ teaspoon salt
½ teaspoon baking powder
½ teaspoon pure vanilla extract
½ teaspoon freshly squeezed lemon juice
¼ cup cold water
2 extra-large eggs
1 cup all-purpose flour, plus more for flouring your work surface
3 cups pastry flour (see Note)
Heaping cup of raspberry jam
½ cup powdered (10X) sugar

1. Position a rack in the center of the oven and preheat to 350°F.
2. Put the shortening, granulated sugar, salt, baking powder, vanilla, and lemon juice in the bowl of a stand mixer fitted with the paddle. (You can use a hand mixer if you allow the shortening to soften at room temperature before beginning.) Start on slow, then increase to medium speed to get out all lumps, about 2 minutes. With the motor running, add the water slowly. Add the eggs one at a time, paddling for 1 minute after each egg. Stop and scrape. Add the all-purpose and pastry flours. Restart the mixer slowly and blend just until the flours are absorbed and the mixture is free of lumps, 2 to 3 minutes.
3. Flour your work surface generously. Divide the dough into two equal pieces and roll half out to a rectangle about 20 by 15 inches and ¼ inch thick. Cut fifteen 4-inch circles with a cookie cutter. Punch 1-inch circles in the center with a punching tool or the back of a #7 pastry tip.
4. Return any scraps to the bowl with the remaining dough and briefly knead together. Roll the dough from the bowl out to form a rectangle about 20 by 15 inches and ¼ inch thick. Cut fifteen 4-inch circles with the same cookie cutter you used in step 3.
5. Line two cookie sheets with parchment paper, using nonstick spray or a dab of butter in each corner to glue the paper in place. Arrange the circles on the sheets. Bake in batches until the edges are golden-brown and the cookies are firm to the touch, 10 to 12 minutes. Remove the cookie sheets from the oven. As soon as the cookies can be moved, use a spatula to transfer them to a rack and let them cool.
6. Spread the bottom cookies (the ones with no holes in the center) with raspberry jam.
7. Sprinkle powdered sugar over the tops (the ones with the holes), then apply one top to each jam-covered base. (Sprinkling the sugar on the tops before affixing them to the cookies ensures the sugar will stay off the jam.)

The cookies may be enjoyed right away, or kept in an airtight container at room temperature for up to 3 days.

These are also delicious spread with the chocolate-hazelnut spread Nutella instead of jam.

Note: You may replace the pastry flour with all-purpose flour but you will lose some elasticity.

Black-and-White Cookies

MAKES 12 COOKIES

Black-and-white cookies, topped with half white fondant and half chocolate, have a deep heritage in New York City, but their popularity has spread over the years, and they're a constant good seller at Carlo's.

If you've ever had a black-and-white cookie, then you might have noticed something different about them. They're spongier than most other cookies, almost springy to the touch. When Mike Vernola, known around Carlo's Bake Shop as Old Man Mike, brought this recipe to the family, he explained to me what made it unique: It's a cake recipe that's been adapted to make a cookie by increasing the ratio of flour to wet ingredients so it doesn't rise as much as a cake would in the oven.

¾ cup plus 2 tablespoons granulated sugar
½ cup (1 stick) unsalted butter
2 extra-large eggs
½ cup milk
¼ teaspoon pure vanilla extract
⅛ teaspoon freshly squeezed lemon juice
1¼ cups cake flour
1¼ cups all-purpose flour
½ teaspoon baking powder
¼ teaspoon salt
¼ cup water
2 cups powdered (10X) sugar
2 tablespoons semisweet chocolate chips or ½ ounce semisweet chocolate,
*   coarsely chopped*

1. Position a rack in the center of the oven and preheat to 340°F.
2. Cream the sugar and butter together in the bowl of a stand mixer fitted with the paddle attachment, starting on low speed and gradually increasing

to medium. (You can use a hand mixer if you let the butter soften at room temperature before beginning.) Add the eggs, one at a time, paddling about 1 minute after each egg is added, then stopping after each one to scrape. Add the milk, vanilla, and lemon juice and paddle just until they are absorbed into the mixture.

3. Sift the cake flour, all-purpose flour, baking powder, and salt together into a separate bowl. Add them to the mixer bowl. Paddle on low speed just until they have been absorbed by the mixture and it is smooth and consistent.

4. Line two cookie sheets with parchment paper, using nonstick spray or a dab of butter in each corner to glue the paper in place.

5. Use a 2-ounce ice cream or ¼-cup measure scoop to scoop batter onto the parchment paper, leaving 2 inches between the cookies.

6. Bake in batches until the cookies are lightly golden brown, about 18 minutes. Remove the cookie sheets from the oven and as soon as the cookies can be moved, use a spatula to transfer them to a rack and let them cool.

7. Transfer the cookies to plates and place in the freezer for about 10 minutes to firm them up.

8. Meanwhile, bring the water to a boil in the top of a double boiler set over simmering water. Whisk in the 10X sugar until the mixture is a uniformly smooth and white. Use a spatula to ice half of the top of each cookie, using the edge of the spatula or the tip of a thin-bladed knife to make a straight edge. (If the icing seizes up, simply return the pot to the double boiler over low heat and whisk to reinvigorate.)

9. Return the pot to the double boiler and stir the chocolate into the remaining icing until it melts and is blended in. Spread the chocolate frosting over the other half of each cookie.

The cookies may be enjoyed right away, or kept in an airtight container at room temperature for up to 3 days.

Why Freeze Before Frosting?

These cookies are frozen before being frosted, to keep their delicate, spongy texture from tearing when you smooth out the fondant. Also, this method won't melt your icing. You can also keep some cookies frozen until ready to ice them. You can adjust the icing, making a thicker one by adding more sugar to the boiling water, or a thinner one by using less sugar.

As with the Seven-Layer Cookies, this technique is a bit of a preview into how we work with full-size cakes, which we also freeze before trimming and frosting (see page 170).

Practice Makes Perfect: Working with Icing

These cookies are frosted with a combination of white and chocolate icings. Working precisely on such a small scale will help prepare you for the larger job of icing entire cakes, and develop your confidence with a spatula.

Icebox Christmas Cookies

MAKES ABOUT 40 COOKIES

Icebox cookies, also sometimes called refrigerator cookies, are popular with home bakers because they can be cut into whatever shapes you like: squares, circles, pinwheels, or anything you can imagine. (Often the final cookies resemble those little butter cookies you see in round tins.) I associate them with Christmas, which is when we always made them at Carlo's Bake Shop, where my dad taught me to make them in our original location on Adams Street. We'd make batch after batch of dough together, and then I'd cut it into holiday shapes such as reindeer, Christmas trees, stars, and bells. Those are the shapes I've featured here, but you can of course make them in whatever shape you like.

By the way, these are as popular now as they've ever been: We sell about 20,000 pounds of them during the month of December alone.

4 cups all-purpose flour, plus more for flouring your work surface and
   hands
1¼ cups vegetable shortening (such as Crisco)
1¼ cups (2½ sticks) unsalted butter
1 cup powdered (10X) sugar
4 extra-large eggs
¼ teaspoon salt
½ cup cold water

1. Put the flour, shortening, butter, sugar, eggs, and salt in the bowl of a stand mixer fitted with the paddle attachment. (You can use a hand mixer if you allow the butter and shortening to soften at room temperature before beginning.)
2. Paddle at low speed until the mixture resembles creamy cookie dough, about 3 minutes; it should be tacky and should not run down the side of the paddle when the motor is stopped. With the motor running on low, slowly add the water and mix until fully absorbed, about 2 minutes more.
3. Wrap the dough in plastic wrap and chill in the refrigerator for 1 hour, or

up to 3 days, but do not freeze. Remove the dough from the refrigerator and let it come to room temperature before proceeding.

4. Position a rack in the center of the oven, and preheat to 325°F.

5. Note that this is a very sticky, difficult dough to handle, so you have to generously flour your work surface and your hands. After flouring, transfer half the dough to your surface and gently roll it into a log, reflouring the top of the dough as necessary as you work to keep it manageable. Work the dough into a 12-inch square, ½ inch thick.

6. Cut about 12 cookies from the first batch (the number will depend on what shape cutter you are using; see headnote), then return the scraps to the bowl, chill again and recut, cutting another 12 or so cookies. Continue to return the scraps to the bowl and repeat with the remaining dough. You will get fewer cookies from each successive batch, and should end with a total of about 40.

7. Arrange the cookies on the cookie sheets, about 1 inch apart, and bake in batches until lightly golden and firm, 12 to 15 minutes.

8. Remove the cookie sheet from the oven. As soon as the cookies can be moved, use a spatula to transfer them to a rack and let them cool.

9. There are a number of options for finishing the cookies:

- To coat with chocolate, melt 2⅔ cups chocolate chips or coarsely chopped chocolate (1 pound of chocolate is a good amount for the number of cookies here) in a double boiler and partially dip the cookies, then let them dry on a rack.
- To coat with colored crystal sugar, spray the cookies lightly with water before baking and dust with red and/or green sugar.
- You can also, of course, leave the cookies plain and they will still be delicious.

Avoid a Sticky Situation

When using a cookie cutter, dip it in flour periodically to keep dough and batters from sticking to it.

What's in a Name?

These are called icebox cookies because the dough is traditionally refrigerated before being cut and baked.

50/50

The recipe calls for equal parts shortening and butter. We originally made it with just shortening, but when I began tinkering with the recipes in the 1990s, I began using butter, which makes the cookies less likely to crumble and contributes their unmistakable flavor.

Pastries

In the development of a baker, if cookies are the childhood phase and cakes are adulthood, then pastries are adolescence, when we transition from one to the other.

In the Carlo's Bake Shop kitchen, pastries are where you take the fundamentals you learned in cookie making to a whole new level. When it comes to pastries, you need to ask more of every part of the process: of the dough, of the bag, and of yourself.

There are more dimensions in play when it comes to pastries. Cookies are, for the most part, flat—almost two dimensional—and with the exception of an occasional icing, or the application of sprinkles, are done once they have been baked and allowed to cool. Many pastries, on the other hand, like cakes, involve an element of design and assembly: The baking is often just one in a series of steps, followed by joining two or more elements and performing delicate piping work.

This chapter features many of my favorite pastries. Some I love for sentimental reasons, like the éclairs that were the first finishing work I ever did, or the butterflies that still bring out the little kid in me. Others I admire for their longevity and ingenuity: my roots may be Sicilian, but I recognize brilliance when I see it, and the French Napoleon (page 93) never fails to amaze me with its simple perfection. Ditto the Cannoli (page 105). We can learn a lot from those two pastries: Just as a great sandwich depends on the right ratio of bread to filling, great pastries have to strike just the right balance between the pastry and the filling, usually cream. In a napoleon, the flaky layers provide just enough support for the light-as-air pastry cream, whereas in a cannoli, a hard shell is called for, not just to carry the dense cream but also to match it with a thick, crunchy counterpart.

Similar considerations come into play when we conceive and make cakes—certain types of frosting require more cake to properly balance them, while others require less. So look at these pastries as more than just a chance to take your skills to the next level; they also offer an opportunity to hone your sense of proportion and balance. Like so much about baking, these are sensibilities that can be developed only through personal experience, by actually doing the work and tasting the results for yourself.

Choux Pastry
Éclair Dough or Cream Puff Dough

MAKES ENOUGH FOR 24 ÉCLAIR OR CREAM PUFF SHELLS

This versatile dough is used for a number of classic pastries, primarily cream puffs and éclairs. It's also the dough used to make French profiteroles.

1 cup water
6 tablespoons (¾ stick) unsalted butter
⅛ teaspoon salt
1 cup all-purpose flour
4 extra-large eggs

1. Put the water, butter, and salt in a heavy saucepan and bring to a boil over high heat. Add the flour and stir with a wooden spoon until the ingredients come together into a smooth, uniform dough, about 2 minutes.
2. Transfer the mixture to the bowl of a stand mixer fitted with the paddle attachment. (You can also use a hand mixer.) Start paddling on low speed, then add the eggs, one at a time, until thoroughly absorbed, mixing for 1 minute between eggs, and stopping the motor periodically to scrape down the sides and bottom of the bowl with a rubber spatula. Finish with the final egg and mix for an additional 2 minutes.

Use the dough immediately. It does not refrigerate well.

Éclairs

MAKES 24 ÉCLAIRS

An éclair is a cousin to the cream puff. Both are made with choux pastry ("pasta choux" or "cream puff dough mix" in the Carlo's Bake Shop vernacular), and both are filled with custard cream. But they have very different characters: Where cream puffs are round, éclairs are shorter and straighter; where cream puffs are finished with, at most, a dusting of powdered sugar, éclairs are topped with poured, melted chocolate.

Cutting and filling éclairs was one of the first jobs I was ever saddled with at Carlo's, where the old pros would cup the shell in one hand and slice though it with a knife held in the other (*please* don't try this at home). It was one of my first and most vivid memories of how a great baker can mimic the timing, efficiency, and exactitude of a machine. Not that I was able to function like that right off the bat; I was so afraid of cutting myself that I would slice away from my body, and make the cut crooked. At home, where you're not concerned with generating hundreds of éclairs in one afternoon, you can simply set the baked éclair on a cutting board and slice it like a piece of bread.

In addition to providing some useful bag work, éclairs will help hone your ability to discern more subtle signs of doneness. Unlike most cookies, which can be assessed with the eyes, éclairs require a gentle assessment by hand; generally speaking, they are done when you can pick one up and have it come off the pan easily.

Choux Pastry (page 88)
3 cups Italian Custard Cream (page 315)
¼ cup water
2 cups powdered (10X) sugar
¼ cup semisweet chocolate chips or 1 ounce semisweet chocolate, coarsely
  chopped

1. Position a rack in the center of the oven and preheat to 450°F.
2. Transfer the dough into a pastry bag fitted with the #6 plain tip. Pipe éclairs

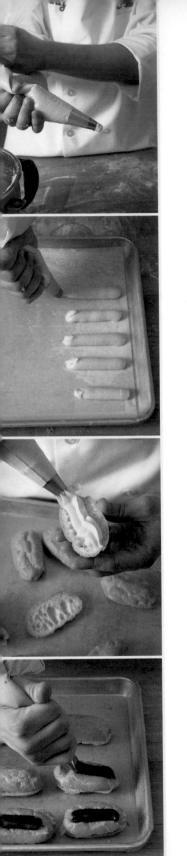

onto nonstick baking trays in strips 1 inch wide and 3 inches long. (You may need more than 2 trays; if so, save some batter until after one tray has been baked, cleared, and cooled.) You should be able to make 24 éclairs.

3. Bake the éclairs in the oven, in batches if necessary, until they are golden brown and they have set enough that you can pick them up (test by gently pinching one with your thumb and forefinger to see if it can be lifted), 15 to 20 minutes. Remove the tray from the oven and let the éclairs cool on the tray for 20 minutes; you don't need to transfer them to a rack to cool. (The éclair shells can be frozen in a plastic freezer bag for up to 1 month; let come to room temperature before cutting and filling.)

4. Working on a cutting board, use a serrated knife to slice the éclairs open like hot dog buns, without cutting all the way through the pastry.

5. Spoon the custard cream into a pastry bag fitted with the #7 star tip. (You can rinse out, dry, and reuse the same bag you used for the dough.) Pipe filling into each éclair.

6. To ice the éclairs, bring the water to a boil in the top of a double boiler set over simmering water. Whisk in the sugar until the mix-

---

Practice Makes Perfect: Steady Pressure

The technique for piping éclairs is called "steady pressure"—it involves squeezing the bag and pulling it to create a line of icing or batter. Éclairs are a great way to practice steady pressure because they use the technique twice: first to pipe the pastry dough, and then to fill the éclairs with cream. (In a cream puff, on the other hand, the technique is "squeeze-and-pull.")

Steady pressure is exactly the same pressure-motion combination used to create swags and drop lines on a cake (see pages 177 and 178). The elders around Carlo's always used to say, "The more pans of éclairs you pull, the better your swags and drop lines will be."

BUDDY VALASTRO

ture is a uniformly smooth and white, then stir in the chocolate until it melts and is blended in. Use an icing spatula to ice the tops of the éclairs. (If the icing seizes up while you're working, simply return the pot to the double boiler over low heat and whisk to reinvigorate.)

Serve the éclairs right away or refrigerate in an airtight container for up to 2 days.

CREAM PUFFS

To make cream puffs instead of éclairs, use the same pastry bag tip. Pipe rounds onto two nonstick baking trays, about 2 inches in diameter by about ½ inch high, leaving 2 inches between puffs. You should be able to make 24 puffs. Bake at the same temperature and for the same length of time.

Fill the puffs either by cutting them in half horizontally with a serrated knife and piping them full of Italian Custard Cream (page 315), or by using your pinkie to hollow out the puffs from the bottom and piping the cream into them through the hole.

Breaking the Rules

I've never believed in blindly following the rules when it comes to baking. Ask most bakers why they do things the way they do, and they'll shrug and tell you, "Because that's the way I was taught." Spend enough time examining *anything* in a bakery and you'll find a way to improve it. That was certainly the case with these éclairs, which break with tradition in two ways. First, rather than piping them full of cream, we slice them open, so the cream sits inside like a hotdog on a bun. This is called an "open éclair" and I think it's more appetizing to look at.

The more dramatic break with tradition is that, rather than using poured chocolate, we top our éclair with icing so it doesn't crack when chilled or bitten into.

Napoleons

We sell thousands of these every Christmas at Carlo's Bake Shop. The original name of this dessert is *millefeuille*, a French word that means "thousand leaves" (*mille foglie* in Italian), a reference to the incredible number of layers in well-made puff pastry. Much as I love homemade everything, this is one case where I urge you to go the store-bought route and make your napoleons with premade puff pastry.

Traditional napoleons are made with three layers of pastry and two layers of cream, but we go a little overboard with four layers of pastry and three of French cream, a mixture of whipped cream and custard. (If you like, you can also make miniature napoleons with just 3 layers of pastry and two of cream.) The pastry is almost just a vehicle for the cream. The topping of marbled vanilla and chocolate icing (see "Creating 'Feathered' Icing," page 95) is wonderful overkill, but for a simple alternative, top this with just powdered sugar.

Pay extra special attention to these when they bake—the effect you're looking for is a light, barely golden brown. If the pastry burns at all, the napoleons will have a burned taste. And here's a trick my dad taught me: To ensure that the napoleons hold together, just before slicing them, set a clean, dry pan on top and press down firmly but gently to be sure the cream and pastry layers are intact; this will also keep the pastry nice and moist and keep it from drying out.

All-purpose flour, for flouring your work surface
2 sheets frozen puff pastry (one 17.3-ounce package, such as Pepperidge Farm), thawed
3 cups Italian Custard Cream (page 315)
2½ cups Italian Whipped Cream (page 321)
¼ cup water
2 cups powdered (10X) sugar
2 tablespoons semisweet chocolate chips or ½ ounce semisweet chocolate, coarsely chopped

1. Position a rack in the center of the oven and preheat to 400°F.
2. Lightly flour your work surface and roll out one puff pastry sheet into a 14 by 12-inch rectangle. Set it on a baking tray and dock it with a fork. (For more, see "Why We Dock Napoleon Dough," below.) Roll out the second sheet and use a pizza cutter to cut a 4 by 14-inch strip and add it to the baking tray alongside the rectangle, docking it with a fork as well. (Return the unused puff pastry to its packaging and return to the freezer.)
3. Bake the puff pastry until it crisps and is very lightly golden all over (the edges will be slightly more golden, but should not be allowed to turn brown), 25 to 35 minutes. Remove the pan from the oven and let cool.
4. Meanwhile, put the custard cream and whipped cream in a mixing bowl and fold together with a rubber spatula to make French cream.
5. Once the pastry has cooled, use a serrated knife to cut the rectangle lengthwise into three 4-inch-wide strips so you have a total of four 4-inch-wide strips.
6. Use a cake icing spatula to spread the cream over one of the strips of puff pastry. Top with another layer and press down gently. Spread the second layer with pastry cream. Top with a third layer of puff pastry and top that with pastry cream.

Why We Dock Napoleon Dough

Though docking pastry dough (poking small holes in it) seems like a casual, random act, there's actually a science to it. The number of perforations affects how much the dough will rise—or not. The holes allow steam to flow between the layers, making the napoleon flaky. If there are no holes, the pastry will simply rise like a soufflé; if there are too many, all the air will escape and it will come out flat.

Docking is done with the tines of a fork. For me, the perfect number of "stabs" for a large rectangle of dough is ten: Imagine each rectangle of puff pastry is a pool table and poke the tines of the fork about where each pocket would be, then dock the dough at four intervals lengthwise down the center of the rectangle.

BUDDY VALASTRO

7. Set the remaining strip of puff pastry on a rack.

8. Bring the water to a boil in the top of a double boiler set over simmering water. Whisk in the sugar until the mixture is uniformly smooth and white. (If the icing seizes up, simply return the pot to the double boiler over low heat and whisk to reinvigorate.) Use a cake icing spatula to ice the strip of puff pastry on the rack.

9. Working quickly, return the pot to the double boiler and stir the chocolate into the remaining icing until it melts and is blended in. Fashion a parchment pencil (see page 185) and carefully spoon some of the warm chocolate into the pencil, first checking to ensure it is not hot enough to burn you. Pipe thin lines of chocolate icing across the vanilla and draw the edge of a paring knife or spatula across it to create a feathered effect. (For more, see "Creating 'Feathered' Icing," below.)

10. Let the icing cool briefly, then top the napoleon with the iced layer, pressing down gently to ensure the layers hold together.

11. Carefully transfer the napoleon to an airtight container and refrig-

Creating "Feathered" Icing

American napoleons are topped with feathered fondant icing. The white base is made by warming water and powdered sugar together and spreading half of it over the napoleon. The chocolate fondant is made by stirring semisweet chocolate into the warm white icing. Make a parchment pencil (see page 185) and spoon the chocolate into it. Use the pencil to draw lines on the white icing with chocolate, then pull the tip of a small, thin-bladed knife, such as a paring knife, across the top to make ripples, 3 inches apart. (You can also accomplish the feathered effect with an icing spatula.)

You can adjust the icing on top of the napoleon to your taste: the more sugar you add, the thicker it will be. You can also omit the icing and top these the way they do in France, with powdered sugar.

erate for at least 1 hour or up to 4 hours (any longer and it will become soggy). When ready to serve, remove the napoleon from the refrigerator and use a serrated knife to slice crosswise into seven 2-inch-wide slices.

If desired, you can skip steps 8 through 10 and simply dust the napoleons with powdered sugar.

Butterflies and *Cassatini*

I've grouped these two pastries together because they show how much is possible in pastry making from the same base recipe. In this case, the recipe produces a sponge-like, cakey pastry that can be used to make both butterflies (pastries shaped like the winged insects for which they're named) or *cassatini*, miniature versions of the traditional Sicilian cassata cake, a spongy cake moistened with liqueur syrup and filled with a ricotta cheese mixture.

The trick to getting these to come out just right is to get the egg whites nice and stiff without overmixing.

Butterfly and *Cassatini* Batter

2 extra-large eggs plus 3 extra-large egg whites
⅓ cup sugar
¼ teaspoon pure vanilla extract
¾ cup plus 2 tablespoons all-purpose flour
Distilled white vinegar, for wiping the bowl
⅛ teaspoon freshly squeezed lemon juice

1. Position a rack in the center of the oven and preheat to 330°F.
2. Put the 2 whole eggs, sugar, and vanilla in the bowl of a stand mixer fitted with the whip attachment and whip on low speed, gradually increasing to medium, until foamy, frothy, and almost ribbony, about 12 minutes. (You can use a hand mixer if you prefer.) Remove the bowl from the machine and fold in the flour with a rubber spatula; the mixture will be pasty, but that's all right. Transfer the mixture to a clean bowl. Wash and dry the mixer bowl, then wipe it with distilled white vinegar to remove all traces of grease and oil.
3. Put the egg whites and lemon juice in the mixer bowl. Whip on low speed

for 2 minutes, then on maximum speed until stiff peaks form, about 5 minutes.

4. Fold one quarter of the whites into the egg-flour mixture, then fold in the rest.

5a. For butterflies: Set paper cupcake cups into 12 wells of a mini muffin tray. Pipe or spoon the batter into the molds up to the top of the papers.

5b. For *cassatini*: Line two baking trays with parchment paper, using nonstick spray or a dab of butter in each corner to glue the paper in place. Put the batter in a pastry bag fitted with a #6 plain tip and pipe 12 rounds of the dough, about 2 inches in diameter by about ½ inch high, leaving 2 inches between puffs.

6. Bake until golden-brown and spongy to the touch, about 20 minutes. (Baking time will be the same for butterflies and *cassatini*.)

7. Remove the tray(s) from the oven and let the pastries cool slightly. For the *cassatini*, use a spatula to transfer them to a rack to cool. Once cooled completely, proceed with the desired finishing touches to make butterflies or *cassatini*.

Folding

When I was a kid, first learning my craft at Carlo's, I was shown how to fold egg whites together with other ingredients in the old-school way, rolling up my sleeve, taking a plastic scraper in hand, and having at it—sticking my arm into an industrial bowl up to the shoulder and working the whites in by hand, achieving something like an intimacy with the whites. At home, you can do this with a rubber spatula; you'll be somewhat removed from the whites, so it's important to pay close visual attention to the changes in the mixture, stopping as soon as the whites are incorporated.

Butterflies

These desserts employ a whimsical bit of design: a conical piece is cut out of the pastry with a paring knife. The inside of the pastry is doused with rum syrup, then filled with custard. The cone is halved and the pieces are stuck in the custard to make little wings. A cherry or strawberry in the center completes the picture.

Don't be discouraged if your first butterflies don't come out just right; the first time I made butterflies, I totally botched them—it's harder than it looks to cut that cone out of the pastry—but as I improved, so did my overall knife skills, which made it all worthwhile.

12 baked Butterfly pastries
1⅓ cups Syrup (page 322), made with light rum
Heaping ¾ cup Italian Custard Cream (page 315)
¼ cup powdered (10X) sugar
12 unhulled strawberry quarters or maraschino cherries

1. Working with one pastry at a time, use a paring knife to cut a conical piece, about ¾ inch deep with a 1-inch-diameter circle at its top, out of the pastry. Repeat with the remaining pastries.
2. Brush rum syrup into the holes and let it soak in.
3. Put the custard cream into a pastry bag fitted with the #7 star tip and pipe cream into the hole, about 1 tablespoon per butterfly.

4. Cut each cone in half across its diameter to make "wings" for the butterflies and set them in the cream.
5. Put the sugar in a sifter and dust the pastries lightly.
6. Set a strawberry quarter where the wings meet on each butterfly, and serve.

Enjoy at once or cover lightly with plastic wrap and refrigerate for up to 2 days.

Cassatini

SICILIAN PASTRIES

When making these, be careful not to lay the icing on too thick; that can lead to a cloying, syrupy effect. This used to happen at the bakery once in a while, until the night I brought a box of *cassatini* to a friend's house for dinner and discovered they were unbearably sweet. After my "talk" with the bakers the next day, the problem never happened again.

Practice Makes Perfect: Assembling

There are times in dessert making when you're not concerned with rolling or piping or baking or decorating, but you'll need to assemble. For theme cakes, whether it's sticking a nose on Frankenstein (page 251) or carving up a Bundt cake and reassembling it as a Thanksgiving Turkey cake (page 255), having a deft set of hands that can use pastry cream as glue and neatly, symmetrically apply pieces to a base is an important skill.

This Italian-American dessert is the perfect way to begin developing touch with a knife, and your skills for assembling pastries and cakes.

BUDDY VALASTRO

12 baked Cassatini pastries
1⅓ cups Syrup (page 322), made with Strega or Rosolio
¼ cup plus 2 tablespoons Cannoli Cream (page 109)
¼ cup water
2 cups powdered (10X) sugar
2 tablespoons assorted minced dried fruit such as cherry, melon, papaya,
  or orange

1. Dig out the inside of all 12 pieces of pastry by hand, leaving just enough that they maintain their shape without collapsing; you want to create half-dome–shaped pieces. Discard (or snack on) the pieces you pulled out.
2. Brush syrup into the inside of each half-dome with a pastry brush and let it soak in.
3. Fill 6 of the pieces with 1 tablespoon cannoli cream.
4. Bring the water to a boil in a double boiler set over simmering water. Whisk in the sugar until the mixture is uniformly smooth and white. Remove the pot from the heat.
5. Sandwich together one filled and one unfilled pastry dome. Dip in the icing, first dipping one half, then carefully dipping the other, holding the pastry with your thumb and forefinger to avoid getting burned. Transfer to a rack to let the icing cool and set. Repeat with the remaining pieces to make 6 *cassatini*.
6. Before the icing dries, top each *cassatini* with 1 teaspoon of the dried fruits.

Enjoy at once or cover lightly with plastic wrap and refrigerate for up to 2 days.

Practice Makes Perfect: Soaking Cakes

Everybody who learns how to soak a cake with syrup has to get over an initial hump: It always seems that there's more syrup than the cake can or should be able to hold. The trick is to learn to brush—almost baste—the cake evenly, adding more syrup as soon as the previous addition has penetrated to the center. Making these pastries is a good way to begin developing a sense of how much syrup a dessert can absorb.

Rum Babas

The rum baba is an irresistible dessert that Italians know from Naples, although it was brought there by French bakers. It's a very simple dessert, and as with any simple recipe, ingredients matter: in this case, the rum itself. I suggest a high-quality light rum for the best flavor and balance.

If you have baba molds, you can by all means use them, but I make them here in a mini muffin or cupcake tray, which is much more common. The trick to making these is learning to manipulate the dough, which is rubbery and stretchy and must be squeezed through your fingers in order to get the desired amount into the wells of the mini muffin or cupcake tray. If you have trouble doing this, an old trick is to dip your fingers in vegetable oil before beginning.

Be sure to generously soak the babas in the syrup; they can look soaked before the syrup has actually penetrated to the center. When you squeeze a properly soaked baba, it should feel like a wet sponge, and liquid should come pouring out.

⅙ cup fresh yeast (see Note)
½ cup lukewarm water
3½ cups all-purpose flour
¼ cup sugar
½ cup vegetable oil
2 tablespoons milk
5 extra-large eggs
Nonstick cooking spray
1⅓ cups Syrup (page 322), made with rum, preferably light
1½ cups Cannoli Cream (page 109) or Italian Custard Cream (page 315)

1. Make a starter by putting the yeast, water, and ½ cup of the flour in a bowl and mix together with your fingers until nicely spongy. Cover the bowl with a damp towel and let proof until doubled in size, about 15 minutes.

2. Put the sugar and oil in the bowl of a stand mixer fitted with the paddle attachment. (You can also use a hand mixer.) Paddle just until blended, then add the milk, then all of the eggs at once. Add the remaining flour and paddle until the mixture comes together, about 5 minutes. Add the starter, scraping and folding to incorporate it. Paddle on medium speed for about 1 minute, then on high speed for 30 seconds.

3. Spray the wells of a mini muffin tray with nonstick spray (even if you're using a nonstick tray).

4. Remove the bowl from the mixer. Put your hand into the bowl and lift out a small handful of dough, then pinch it between your thumb and forefinger, causing a small blob to form. Working quickly to prevent the blob from dropping, guide the dough with the blob on top into a well of the mini muffin tray and deposit it inside. (The dough should not come all the way up the sides of the well.) Continue until you have filled all 24 wells.

5. Cover the tray with a damp towel and let proof in a cool, dry place for half an hour or until the dough has about doubled in size.

6. Meanwhile, position a rack in the center of the oven and preheat to 350°F.

7. Bake the babas until lightly golden-brown and springy to the touch, about 20 minutes. Remove the tray from the oven and let them cool.

8. Pour the syrup into a small, heavy pot and heat over low heat to 140°F. Remove the pot from the heat and, working with one at a time, lower the babas into the pot, holding the bottom and dipping the wider top into the syrup. Let sit in the syrup for 5 minutes, then lift out, squeeze gently to release any extra syrup, and let rest on a baking tray or large plate for a few minutes to allow any excess syrup to drain out.

9. Put the cream in a pastry bag (you do not need a tip in this case). Slice each baba in half vertically with a serrated knife and pipe full of cream.

The babas may be enjoyed right away or may be covered loosely with plastic wrap and refrigerated for up to 2 days.

Note: If you cannot find fresh yeast, or would rather use active dry yeast, use 1 packet (2¼ teaspoons) active dry yeast and start the recipe by pouring the packet into a heat-proof vessel. Heat ¼ cup water over low heat until warm but not truly hot or boiling. Pour it over the yeast, add 1 teaspoon sugar, and stir. Let the mixture sit until foamy, about 5 minutes. Proceed with step 1, lowering the amount of water added to ¼ cup.

Cannoli

This is the Carlo's Bake Shop recipe for authentic cannoli; we still make them with the recipe my father retained from his family's bakery back in the Old Country. Consider making these in larger batches; because of the way the shells are fried in the lard they are able to stay preserved, so you can save them for a long time and fill when you're ready to serve them.

Take care to get the tip deep into the cannoli when you pipe these full of cream — the most common cannoli mistake made at Carlo's is when a young baker doesn't fill them all the way to the center. When I used to make that mistake as a kid, my Dad took a spoon and filled the cannoli the rest of the way, and I still have to do the same thing on occasion.

Notes: You will need four 6-inch-long, ¾- to 1-inch-diameter wooden dowels. You can replace the lard for frying with vegetable shortening; the exact amount will depend on the size of your pot

1 cup all-purpose flour, plus more for flouring the dough and your work
surface
3 tablespoons granulated sugar
2 tablespoons leaf lard, plus enough for frying (see "Why Lard?" page 108)
2 tablespoons distilled white vinegar
2 extra-large eggs
¼ teaspoon ground cinnamon
¼ teaspoon fine sea salt
3 cups Cannoli Cream (page 109)
Powdered (10X) sugar, for dusting the cannoli

1. Put the flour, granulated sugar, 2 tablespoons of the lard, the vinegar, 1 egg, the cinnamon, and salt in the bowl of a stand mixer fitted with the hook attachment. Mix on low-medium speed until well combined, approximately

10 minutes. (There is no need to stop the motor to scrape the sides because this dough will pull together into a ball when it's ready.)

2. Remove the dough from the bowl, wrap it in plastic wrap, and let it rest at room temperature for at least 30 minutes or up to 3 hours, to soften the dough and make it less elastic.

3. Lightly coat the dough with flour and roll it through a pasta machine set to the thickest setting (usually number 1). If you do not have a pasta machine, use a rolling pin to roll the dough out as thin as possible on a lightly floured surface, to no more than ⅛ inch thick. Make 5-inch-long ovals from the dough (see "Shaping Cannoli," below). Gather up the excess dough, knead it together, roll it out, and cut ovals again. You should have 10 ovals.

4. Beat the remaining egg in a small bowl. Fill a wide, deep, heavy pot two-thirds full of lard (the pot should be wide and/or deep enough to hold four dowels without crowding or touching) and set over medium-high heat. Heat the lard to 350°F to 375°F. Line a large plate or platter with paper towels.

5. Wrap one oval lengthwise around a 6-inch-long, ¾- to 1-inch-diameter wooden dowel. Be very careful to wrap it loosely, leaving a little space between the dowel and the pastry dough so that, when fried, the inside will be cooked as well. Use a pastry brush to paint one end of the shell with egg. Pull the egg-brushed end over the opposite end, and press them together, sealing the shell around the dowel. (To speed the egg-washing process you can do as we do at Carlo's and arrange the shells in overlapping fashion, then brush egg wash on the "lips" as shown.) Repeat with two more dowels and shells.

Shaping Cannoli

How to make the trademark cannoli shape: Use a 4-inch round cookie cutter (or the mouth of a 4-inch bowl) to punch circles out of the dough. Working with one circle at a time, grasp the circles at the 3 o'clock and 9 o'clock positions and gently pull into an oval 5 inches long. If you plan to make a lot of cannoli, you can also bend a round cookie cutter into an oval shape by pressing on it from two sides.

6. Carefully lower the dowels into the oil and fry the shells until golden-brown, turning them with a slotted spoon as they fry, approximately 10 minutes. Use the spoon to carefully remove the dowels from the lard and transfer them to the paper towel–lined plate to cool.
7. When the shells are cool enough to touch, approximately 10 minutes, pull the dowels out.
8. Repeat shaping, frying, and cooling for two more batches, frying three more in the second batch, and four in the last, until all shells have been fried and removed from the dowels.
9. When ready to fill and serve the cannoli, put the cannoli cream in a pastry bag fitted with the #7 plain tip. Carefully insert the tip halfway into one shell and pipe the cream in, pulling the tip out to fill all the way to the end. Insert the tip in the other side of the shell, to the center, and pipe and pull again to ensure the shell is completely filled from end to end. Repeat with the remaining shells.
10. Dust the finished cannoli with powdered sugar and serve.

The shells may be held in an airtight container at room temperature for up to 3 months. I urge you not to fill the cannoli more than 1 hour before serving: They may become soggy.

Don't Feel Like Frying?

You can purchase cannoli shells and fill them with the Cannoli Cream.

Why Lard?

The best, most authentic cannoli are made with lard and fried in lard. You can use vegetable shortening instead, but if you want that resilient crunch and classic flavor that you associate with cannoli from Carlo's or another true Italian bakery, you need lard.

Cannoli Cream

MAKES ABOUT 3 CUPS

This is the classic ricotta-based filling for cannoli. It's also wonderful for filling Rum Babas (page 103) or as a cake filling (see page 171). If you can find cocoa drops, replace the chocolate chips with them; they are made specifically for cannoli cream.

2 cups fresh ricotta
⅔ cup granulated sugar
¼ teaspoon ground cinnamon
⅓ cup semisweet chocolate chips, preferably mini chips

1. Put the ricotta, sugar, and cinnamon in the bowl of a stand mixer fitted with the paddle attachment. (If you don't have a stand mixer you can use a hand mixer.) Paddle on low to medium speed until the sugar is completely dissolved, 2 to 3 minutes. The best way to tell if it's dissolved is to taste the mixture until you don't detect any graininess. Take care not to overmix, or the mixture will become soft and runny.
2. Add the chips and paddle just until evenly distributed, approximately 30 seconds. Stop to keep from breaking up the chips.

Use the cream immediately or refrigerate in an airtight container for up to 5 days.

Brownies

Who doesn't love a brownie? Rich and fudgy, these are made in the classic way, with a recipe from Old Man Mike. (Mike made his with nuts, but we've cut back on those, owing to the increasing number of allergies out there today.)

One of the signature flourishes of these brownies grew out of something we do for practical reasons: when we turn a pan of brownies over onto parchment paper, we sugar the top so it doesn't stick to the parchment. The sugar creates a bit of a crust that makes an impression, even if you top the brownies with the fudge icing.

Trust your sense of timing when you make brownies: For them to be fudgy, you have to take them out of the oven in an almost raw state.

1 cup plus 1 tablespoon sugar
½ cup (1 stick) unsalted butter
4 extra-large eggs
2 cups chocolate syrup
1 cup all-purpose flour
Nonstick spray, for the baking tray
Brownie Icing (recipe follows; optional)

1. Position a rack in the center of the oven and preheat to 325°F.
2. Cream 1 cup sugar and the butter in the bowl of a stand mixer fitted with the paddle attachment. (You can use a hand mixer if you allow the butter to soften at room temperature before beginning.) Paddle on low speed, then medium, for a total of 2 to 3 minutes. Add the eggs all at once, and paddle at low speed until blended, about 1 minute. Add the syrup and paddle for another minute; the mixture will be very wet, but that's okay. Paddle on low speed for about 1 minute, then stop and scrape. Add the flour, paddle on low for 1 minute, then scrape. Paddle on low until thoroughly mixed; the mixture will still be very wet and look a little grainy.

3. Spray a 13 by 9 by 2-inch-deep baking tray with nonstick spray and line the bottom with parchment paper. Pour the batter into the pan. It won't even come halfway up the sides, and that's all right.
4. Bake until crispy on top, the batter begins to pull away from the sides of the pan, and a toothpick inserted to the center comes out clean, about 30 minutes.
5. Remove the tray from the oven and let the brownies cool in the pan. Cover a cutting board with parchment paper. Sprinkle the brownies with the remaining 1 tablespoon sugar and gently turn the brownies out onto the parchment paper by inverting the tray. Peel off the parchment if it is stuck to the brownies.
6. If desired, ice the brownies using an offset spatula and let the icing cool and stiffen.
7. Cut the brownies into 6 even strips (1½ inches each) along the length of the batch, then crosswise at 3¼-inch intervals to make 24 brownies.

The brownies should be enjoyed as soon as possible, but can be refrigerated in an airtight container for up to 3 days. They may also be frozen for up to 1 month; let come to room temperature before serving.

Brownie Icing

Use this fudgy icing to decadently coat brownies.

1¼ cups sugar
6 tablespoons (¾ stick) unsalted butter
6 tablespoons whole milk
1 cup semisweet chocolate chips or coarsely chopped semisweet chocolate
(6 ounces)

1. Put the sugar, butter, and milk in a pot and bring to a boil, stirring, over medium-high heat.
2. Remove the pot from the heat and whisk in the chocolate until melted.
3. Let the mixture cool slightly, then ice the brownies while the icing is soft and pliable. Use right away; do not let stiffen, and do not store.

Raspberry Bars

One of the great bakers in Carlo's history, Jimmy Lee, taught me to make these elegant bars when I was a teenager. The technique is simple—you fashion logs of dough, then form a ravine in the center into which jam is spread before baking.

These should be made with bake-proof jam, but if you can't find it, you can bake the bars without the jam, then spread them with jam after they've cooled. The better the jam, the better the bars will be: A salesman once tried to sell me on a cheaper brand of jam and, like any good businessman, I was happy to give it a try, but the bars were simply gross and I've never tried an alternative brand again.

1 cup (2 sticks) butter
½ cup sugar
1 tablespoon milk
1 extra-large egg
2½ cups pastry flour (no substitutions)
All-purpose flour, for your work surface
¾ cup bake-proof raspberry jam (see headnote)

1. Position a rack in the center of the oven and preheat to 350°F.
2. Starting on low speed and gradually increasing to medium, cream the butter and sugar in the bowl of a stand mixer fitted with the paddle attachment. Add the milk and egg and continue to paddle until the mixture is smooth, 2 to 3 minutes on low speed, stopping the motor to scrape with a rubber spatula about halfway through.
3. Stop the motor, lower the bowl, and add the pastry flour all at once. Paddle on medium speed for 1 minute, then increase to high. Continue to paddle just until the mixture is smooth and homogeneous.
4. Flour your work surface and transfer the dough to the surface. Cut the

dough into thirds. Roll each third out into a block about 12 inches long and 3 inches wide.

5. Line two 13 by 9-inch baking trays with parchment paper, using nonstick spray or a dab of butter in each corner to glue the paper in place. Arrange the blocks on the pans (2 in one pan and 1 in the other), with several inches of space between them. Use your fingers to make a ravine in the center of each one, pressing down on the dough. Spread the jam out along the ravines.

6. Bake until the bars are golden-brown, 18 to 22 minutes.

7. Remove the trays from the oven. As soon as the bars can be moved, use a spatula to transfer them to a rack and let them cool. Transfer to a cutting board and cut the bars crosswise into 4 pieces per bar.

Enjoy the bars right away or refrigerate in an airtight container for up to 4 days. Whole bars, with the jam on them, can be wrapped loosely in plastic wrap and frozen, then thawed and cut.

Old-Fashioned Doughnuts

MAKES 12 DOUGHNUTS AND 12 OR MORE HOLES

My father didn't make doughnuts all the time at Carlo's Bake Shop, but he had a great recipe for them, and made them once in a while as a special treat. That's how I think of them at home—it's unlikely that you'll make these as often as, say, pancakes or waffles, but as an occasional indulgence, they're a wonderful thing to have in your repertoire. They're great on weekends, and especially perfect for winter holiday get-togethers when the festive aroma of cinnamon will fill the house.

How you make doughnuts in a professional bakery gives away your age. The old-timers at Carlo's used a machine called a Dutchess (named for the manufacturer) that cut the dough into little rectangles; the guys would make a hole in the center and fold the doughnut through itself, then douse it in flour. When it hit the hot oil, it magically turned into a doughnut thanks to the way the shape and the flour interacted with the oil. Guys my age use a dropper, but when I showed up with it one day, I thought the veterans were going to kill me.

At home, there are two shapes I recommend: one is the classic tire shape, produced by punching circles of the dough and then punching out the center. The other is the Mae West, named for its curvaceous shape, which is described in the variation.

But don't be married to the shape; you can make these in whatever shape you like.

3 cups all-purpose flour, plus more for flouring your work surface and
  hands
1 cup granulated sugar
¾ cup buttermilk
2 extra-large eggs
2 tablespoons vegetable shortening (such as Crisco)
2 teaspoons baking powder
1 teaspoon baking soda
1 teaspoon salt

½ teaspoon ground cinnamon
About 2 quarts vegetable oil, for frying
About 1 cup powdered (10X) sugar, for dusting (see "Finishing
Touches," page 118)

1. Put 1½ cups of the flour in the bowl of a stand mixer fitted with the paddle attachment. (You can use a hand mixer instead if you use a rubber spatula to fold in the flour in step 2.) Add the granulated sugar, buttermilk, eggs, shortening, baking powder, baking soda, salt, and cinnamon. Start the mixer slowly to avoid spraying the flour. After 30 seconds, stop and scrape with a rubber spatula, then paddle on medium speed until blended together with no lumps, 1 to 1½ minutes.

2. Add the remaining flour gradually (holding it out until this time, which keeps lumps from forming) to avoid spraying flour. After 30 seconds, stop and scrape with a rubber spatula. Mix on medium speed until blended together with no lumps, 1 to 1½ minutes. It will resemble aerated cookie dough.

3. Wrap the dough in plastic wrap and chill in the refrigerator for at least 1 hour or up to 3 days, but do not freeze. Let it come to room temperature before proceeding.

4. Note that this is a very sticky, difficult dough to handle, so you have to generously flour your work surface and your hands. After doing so, transfer half the dough to your surface and gently knead it, flouring the top of the dough as necessary as you work to keep it manageable. Work the dough into a 7-inch square, ½ inch thick, rolling it out gently with a pin to smooth the top. Fold the dough in thirds, like a letter, flour the work surface and the dough, and roll over it again with the pin to form a 7-inch square.

5. Punch about five 3-inch circles out of the dough with a doughnut cutter. If you do not have a doughnut cutter, use a 3-inch cookie cutter and an inverted pastry tip (with a 1-inch diameter at the wide end) to punch out the center of each circle.

6. Add the scraps to the reserved dough and repeat steps 4 and 5, making another 5 doughnuts. Reroll the scraps ½ inch thick and cut another doughnut. You should get fewer doughnuts from each successive batch, and should end with a total of about 12. If you have any extra dough, but not enough to make another doughnut, you can make doughnut holes instead, punching them out with the pastry tip

BAKING WITH THE CAKE BOSS

and rolling them by hand into spheres the size of a Ping-Pong ball.

7. Transfer the doughnuts to a plate or a sheet of waxed paper, gently shaking them free of flour, which can dirty the frying oil.

8. Fill a pot at least 6 inches deep and at least 10 inches wide, with vegetable oil to a depth of 1½ inches. Heat over low heat to 350°F. Cover a platter or tray with paper towels.

9. Lower the doughnuts into the oil in batches of three or four, taking care not to drop them from too high (this can cause the hot oil to splash). Fry, using a wooden spoon to gently turn the doughnuts over twice, until they are dark golden on each side and they feel spongy when you press against them with the spoon (don't be afraid to let them get good and dark if necessary), about 2 minutes. Don't overfry or they will become hard. Remove the doughnuts with the spoon and drain on the paper towels. Repeat with the remaining doughnuts, letting the oil return to 350°F between batches. (It is best to change the oil after every 12 doughnuts.)

10. Once they are cool, dust the doughnuts with the powdered sugar by putting the sugar in a sifter and sifting it over them.

The sooner these are eaten, the better, but they may be stored in an airtight container at room temperature for up to 24 hours.

Finishing Touches

You can also dust the doughnuts with cinnamon sugar, made by stirring together 2 cups granulated sugar and 2 tablespoons ground cinnamon. Put the mixture in a bowl and roll the doughnuts in it. This is the traditional coating for Mae West doughnuts.

BUDDY VALASTRO

Mae West Doughnuts

1. After forming doughnuts, cut each doughnut and straighten it out. Roll it out to a cord 15 inches long and ½ inch in diameter.
2. Fold the cord in half and press the halves together. Take each end in one hand and twist in opposing directions, as though wringing a towel, to form a twisty, cruller-like shape.
3. Gently press down on the ends to hold the shape.
4. Fry the doughnuts for about 1 minute total cooking time, flipping them three or four times with a wooden spoon in one quick, deft movement to keep them from overbrowning. Remove the finished doughnuts from the oil with two spoons.

This recipe will also produce 12 doughnuts.

Munchkins

You can make doughnut holes, aka Munchkins, by punching 1-inch circles out of the dough and rolling them into balls. Fry in batches of 8 to 10, frying for about 1 minute, turning them once during that time, and removing them from the oil with a slotted spoon. This recipe will yield about 96 Munchkins.

Practice Makes Perfect: Making Doughnuts

These two variations of doughnut making offer a progression in their own right. The classic, hole-in-the-middle doughnut shape is very forgiving because the hole ensures even cooking, allowing oil to bathe the dough from the outside and the center. The long, double-helix shape of a Mae West is more challenging—the oil temperature has to be just right, and the doughnut has to be turned more often to ensure correct and even cooking. So learn your doughnut making with the classic shape, then graduate to the Mae West.

Chocolate Truffles

These miniature flourless chocolate tortes are sinfully rich and super easy to make. If you like, you can skip the ganache and top each truffle with a scoop of ice cream.

Take care not to overwhip the egg whites or they will break down.

1 cup (2 sticks) unsalted butter
½ cup (1 stick) margarine
3¼ cups semisweet chocolate chips or 1½ pounds semisweet chocolate,
  coarsely chopped
3 extra-large eggs, separated
Nonstick spray, for the cupcake tray
2 cups Chocolate Ganache (page 318)
24 raspberries
About 4 cups Chocolate Fudge Frosting (page 313)
4 ounces white chocolate

1. Position a rack in the center of the oven and preheat to 320°F.
2. In a small pot, melt the butter and margarine over medium heat. Once melted, remove the pot from the heat and stir in the chocolate with a rubber spatula until melted, then stir in the egg yolks. Set aside.
3. Put the egg whites in a very clean bowl (see page 56 for notes on whipping egg whites) and whip until stiff peaks form. Fold in the chocolate mixture.
4. Spray the wells of a cupcake tray with nonstick spray. Pour ⅓ cup of the mixture into each well.
5. Bake until the truffles rise up over the top of the wells like little soufflés and start to crack at the top. Remove the tray from the oven and let cool completely before unmolding them; the truffles will drop. (If you want to speed the process, after they have cooled slightly, put the cupcake tray in the refrigerator.)

6. Unmold the truffles and pour the ganache into the sunken tops, about 1 tablespoon per truffle.
7. Top each truffle with 2 raspberries.
8. Put the frosting in a pastry bag fitted with the #32 tip and pipe rosettes (see page 181) around the edge of the truffles. (You will not use all the frosting.) This is most easily done on a turntable following the instructions on page 152.
9. Melt the white chocolate in the top of a double boiler set over simmering water. Dip the tines of a fork in the chocolate and drizzle the chocolate over the truffles.

The truffles are best eaten right away.

Pies and Tarts

In the education of a baker and decorator, pies and tarts are funny things. In some ways, they seem disconnected from other categories of baked goods because they are constructed differently from everything else: usually as a shell with cream, fruit, custard, or some other filling.

But pies and tarts are actually the perfect bridge between making cookies and pastries and making the quantum leap to cakes because they offer crucial lessons in two areas: working on a larger scale and developing your own personal style of design and decorating. Even something as basic as a Lemon Meringue Pie (page 127) offers a chance to experiment with a piping bag, trying out different effects every time you apply the meringue to a new pie.

On a deeper level, making a dessert like *Frutti di Bosco* (page 145), starts training your eyes and hands to work together to make something distinctly beautiful and distinctly "you"—the ratios of the different fruits to each other and how you arrange them on the tart are things that no two bakers do the same way; every time you make it, you'll find yourself making adjustments until you hit on your own signature version. A Cream Puff Parfait (page 147) presents similar options—whether you finish it with cocoa powder, chocolate shavings, a drizzle of melted chocolate, or all three is entirely up to you, and how you integrate the effects, or make one stand out on its own, is something each baker has to figure out to best reflect his or her own vision. I learned that dessert from my father, who invented it at Carlo's. He made the parfait differently every time, basing it on his mood or on new ideas, like adding espresso beans as a finishing touch. When I began making the parfait, I naturally mimicked his style, but in time began to develop my own parfait style, just as I did for any dessert that invited personal expression.

From a technical standpoint, pies and cakes might not look very similar, but there are skills called for in pie making that will help you when it comes time to make cakes. For example, rolling and cutting the lattice to top a wheat pie (page 137) is the closest thing to working with fondant you will encounter outside of actually doing it. Ditto rolling out a pie crust, which uses exactly the

same technique, including the final step of rolling the dough up on the pin, then unspooling it over the shell.

Of course, all of this is the icing on the . . . well, on the pie, I guess. Do you really need a reason to make any of the desserts I just named, or the other ones in this chapter, such as apple and pumpkin pie, two classics that I can never get enough of? I hope not. But then again, at the same time, I hope that your increasing mastery of all parts of the baking process makes the end result taste just a little sweeter each step of the way.

Lemon Meringue Pie

MAKES ONE 9-INCH PIE, ENOUGH TO SERVE 10 TO 12

If you're new to baking and looking to develop some baseline comfort, a lemon meringue pie is a good place to start because you don't bake the filling in the pie. Instead, you make the crust, lemon curd filling, and meringue separately, then assemble them. So you only need to be able to successfully bake the crust to pull this off. The only other baking is a quick flash in the oven to caramelize the crystal sugar that we dust the meringue with at the end. (We originally used powdered sugar, but have changed it over the years.)

Because it was his wife's favorite dessert, the late, great Carlo's baker Sal Picinich used to say, "If you bring home lemon meringue pie, you get lucky!" I hear it also works well for getting a man out of the doghouse.

½ cup cornstarch
1½ plus ⅓ cups water
4 extra-large eggs, separated
½ cup freshly squeezed lemon juice
2 cups granulated sugar
1¼ teaspoons salt
3 tablespoons unsalted butter
2 teaspoons finely grated lemon zest
Distilled white vinegar, for wiping the bowl
1 Pie Crust (page 130), blind baked
1 tablespoon crystal sugar (optional)

1. Put the cornstarch and ⅓ cup water in a small bowl and stir them together.
2. Put the egg yolks and lemon juice in another bowl and whisk them together.
3. Put 1½ cups of the sugar, 1 teaspoon of the salt, and 1½ cups water in a small, heavy saucepan and set it over medium-high heat. Bring to a boil, then whisk in the cornstarch mixture. Continue to whisk until the mixture

becomes thick and clear, then whisk in the lemon-yolk mixture. Continue to whisk until the mixture boils and thickens, about 3 minutes.

4. Remove the pan from the heat and whisk in the butter and lemon zest. Set aside.

5. Clean the bowl of a stand mixer fitted with the whip attachment with vinegar. (You can also use a hand mixer.) Add the egg whites and ¼ teaspoon salt and start whipping on low speed. Once the mixture becomes frothy, add the remaining ½ cup sugar and continue to whip until stiff peaks form, gradually increasing the speed to high, about 5 minutes. If you add the sugar too early, it slows the peaks' formation.

6. Preheat the oven to 325°F.

7. Transfer the lemon filling to the pie crust. Spread half the meringue over the top with a spatula.

8. Transfer the rest of the meringue into a pastry bag fitted with the #7 star tip or French tip and pipe the meringue on top. (See "Practice Makes Perfect: Express Yourself," below).

Practice Makes Perfect: Express Yourself

What can you learn about yourself from a lemon meringue pie? When it comes to decorating, more than you might think. Because how you pipe meringue has no effect on flavor, any desserts using meringue are a terrific opportunity for low-risk experimentation. During the holidays at Carlo's Bake Shop, when we produced dozens of these pies every day, I used to try different styles and designs—making puffs with a pastry bag, or hitting globs of meringue with a knife to make it spiky, which became the bakery's signature presentation. (This particular motion can also be used to spike chocolate fudge frosting.) I never did two pies exactly the same way, and the exercise helped me get a sense of what worked and what didn't and to develop my own intuition and personal style.

Whenever you are making this pie, try something a little different. Have *fun*. If you own a turntable, you can do as I did when I was a kid and get some practice using it as well.

9. If using, sprinkle the crystal sugar over the meringue.
10. Put the pie on a baking tray and finish in the oven just until the meringue is singed, about 12 minutes.
11. Remove the pie from the oven and let cool.

Serve at once, or cover loosely with plastic wrap and refrigerate for up to 3 days.

Pie Crust

MAKES ONE 9-INCH PIE CRUST

There's nothing wrong with buying a prepared pie crust, but it's so easy to make your own that I urge you to do so whenever possible.

2 cups all-purpose flour, plus more for flouring your work surface
¾ cup vegetable shortening (such as Crisco)
1 tablespoon sugar
1 teaspoon fine sea salt
7 tablespoons ice-cold water (see recipe step 1)

1. Put the flour, shortening, sugar, and salt in the bowl of a stand mixer fitted with the paddle attachment. Paddle at the lowest speed just until the mixture holds together, about 30 seconds. (You can use a hand mixer if you allow the shortening to soften at room temperature before beginning.) Add 6 tablespoons water, and paddle until absorbed, about 30 seconds. If the dough seems dry or fails to come together, add the last tablespoon of water.
2. Transfer the dough to a piece of plastic wrap and refrigerate for 30 to 60 minutes.

Blind Baking

If you need to bake the crust with no filling, fill the crust with dry beans or rice, or set another pie pan in the well, invert the whole assemblage onto a baking tray, and bake on the center rack of an oven preheated to 350°F until the crust is firm and golden, about 25 minutes.

BUDDY VALASTRO

3. Lightly flour your work surface, and roll out the dough in a circle about 14 inches in diameter (see "How to Measure for a Pie Pan Without a Ruler," below) and about ¼ inch thick. Roll it up onto the rolling pin (see "How to Roll Pastry onto a Rolling Pin," below), and transfer to a 9-inch pie pan, unspooling it over the top. Tap the pan gently on the work surface and the dough will fall into place. Put your hands at the 2 o'clock and 10 o'clock positions on the side of the pan, and rotate the pan from just under the lip to cause the excess dough to fall away. (If molded in an aluminum pie pan, the dough can be wrapped in plastic and frozen for up to 2 months. Let thaw to room temperature before filling and baking.)

Note: If you are making this in the summer, use 6 tablespoons water to account for increased humidity affecting the moisture content of the flour.

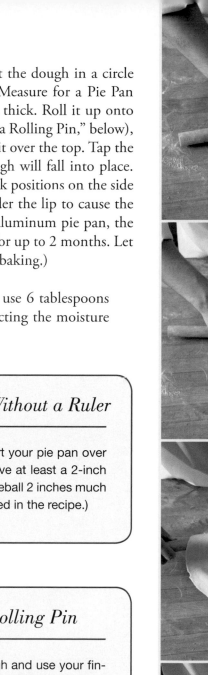

How to Measure for a Pie Pan Without a Ruler

If you don't have a ruler in the kitchen, invert your pie pan over the dough, centering it, making sure you have at least a 2-inch border of dough around the pan. (You can eyeball 2 inches much more accurately than the 14 inches mentioned in the recipe.)

How to Roll Pastry onto a Rolling Pin

Put the rolling pin at the far side of the dough and use your fingers to coil it around the pin, then simply roll it up onto the pin.

Pumpkin Pie

MAKES ONE 9-INCH PIE, ENOUGH TO SERVE 10 TO 12

I think there's no more American category of desserts than pies, ready to reflect the seasons with berries and stone fruits in the summer, and autumn bounty in the fall and winter. The first pie I think of is pumpkin pie because that's the one that's associated with Thanksgiving, when we make more pies in one week at Carlo's than we do the rest of the year combined.

You might be surprised that we use canned pumpkin for this recipe, and that I suggest you do the same at home. The reason is simply that fresh pumpkin is too variable and watery to behave right in a pie, let alone enable you to follow a recipe with any consistency.

One 15-ounce can pumpkin puree (I like Libby's Pure Pumpkin)
¾ cup sugar
1½ teaspoons cornstarch
½ teaspoon fine sea salt
1 teaspoon ground cinnamon
¼ teaspoon ground cloves
¼ teaspoon ground ginger
¼ teaspoon ground nutmeg
¼ teaspoon ground allspice
¼ teaspoon ground mace
1 teaspoon pure vanilla extract
1½ cups whole milk
2 extra-large eggs
1 unbaked 9-inch Pie Crust, homemade (page 130) or store-bought

1. Position a rack in the center of the oven and preheat to 450°F.
2. Put the pumpkin, sugar, cornstarch, salt, cinnamon, cloves, ginger, nutmeg, allspice, mace, and vanilla in the bowl of a stand mixer fitted with the paddle attachment. Paddle at low-medium speed for approximately 2 minutes.

3. With the motor running, pour in the milk in two additions. Stop the motor, scrape the sides of the bowl with a wooden spatula, restart, and paddle for an additional 2 minutes. Add the eggs and paddle until absorbed, approximately 2 additional minutes.

4. Pour the mixture into a 9-inch pie crust in a pan and bake for 15 minutes, then lower the heat to 375°F and bake until a finger dabbed onto the surface emerges clean, 30 to 40 minutes.

5. Remove the pie from the oven and let cool for 1 to 2 hours.

   Slice and serve right away, or cover with plastic wrap and refrigerate for up to 3 days.

Coconut Custard Pie

MAKES ONE 9-INCH PIE, ENOUGH TO SERVE 10 TO 12

Coconut custard pie is a real crowd-pleaser that blends a rich filling with the light flavor and fragrance of shredded coconut—the combination always reminds me of a tropical vacation, or of a piña colada, minus the pineapple. It happens to be my sister Mary's favorite dessert. It's also one of the last recipes that Sal and I reformulated together. We had to address an occasional problem: The custard had a tendency to erupt like a volcano in the oven. Adding some more heavy cream to the recipe calmed the mixture down and stopped that from happening.

Be very careful when filling this pie, a step that you complete while the pie is in the oven. At Carlo's, we still use an ancient, hand-crafted tool—a broomstick onto which a pot has been tied. For all of the modern equipment and technology that have been devised in the past decades, this remains the best, safest way to do it. At home, pouring the filling from a measuring cup is the best way to go.

1 unbaked 9-inch Pie Crust (page 130) with the edges crimped (see the
*   instructions in the Apple Pie recipe, page 141)*
4 extra-large eggs
¾ cup plus 2 tablespoons sugar
⅓ cup cornstarch
1 cup heavy cream
¼ teaspoon pure vanilla extract
Pinch ground nutmeg
1½ cups warm milk
1 cup unsweetened shredded coconut

1. If making your own pie crust, inspect it to be sure there are no holes or tears; the custard filling is added in liquid form and if there's a hole, it will leak out.
2. Position a rack in the center of the oven and preheat to 400°F.

3. Put the eggs, sugar, and cornstarch in a bowl and whisk them together. Add the heavy cream gradually, while whisking. Whisk in the vanilla, nutmeg, and milk.

4. Put the pie pan on a baking tray. Sprinkle the coconut into the bottom of the pie pan, being sure to do it evenly.

5. Pour in enough of the custard to come three quarters of the way up the sides of the pie pan. As you pour in the custard, the coconut will rise; use a toothpick to stir the custard and evenly distribute it, being careful not to cut into the bottom of the pie crust. Transfer the remaining custard into a Pyrex measuring cup or other heatproof, spouted vessel.

6. Put the tray on the middle rack of the oven. Pour in enough custard to come just up to the top of the pie pan. (You may have extra custard; don't worry if you do but don't overfill the pie pan.)

7. Bake until the top of the pie is golden and doesn't shake at all when you agitate the pan, 30 to 35 minutes. Remove the tray from the oven and let the pie cool, then cover loosely with plastic wrap and chill in the refrigerator for at least 1 hour.

The pie may be served at once, or refrigerated for up to 2 days.

Pastiera di Grano
Wheat Pie

MAKES ONE 10-INCH PIE, ENOUGH TO SERVE 10 TO 12

This Italian Easter specialty is my favorite pie because there's nothing else like it. Made with wheat berries that are boiled down, enriched with butter, and enlivened with orange blossom water, it has an orangey, citrusy, floral flavor.

I was taught how to make this pie by my grandmother Grace, who used to say to me, "Make sure you cook it nice, the wheat has to be cooked nice inside, darker than lighter." We don't make as many of these as we used to because the younger generation doesn't really know wheat pie, and it looks different from any other type of pie. And I have to admit, if I didn't know this pie myself, and saw it in the pastry case, I'd pick an apple pie over it any day of the week. But since I know it, I love it; I also love tasting the raw mix (even though it has raw egg yolk in it).

1 pound ricotta cheese
1 cup sugar
3 tablespoons orange blossom water
½ teaspoon finely grated lemon zest
½ teaspoon finely grated orange zest
3 extra-large eggs
1 pound cooked wheat berries, cooled (about 3 cups)
1 unbaked 10-inch Pasta Frolla *(recipe follows)*

1. Position a rack in the center of the oven and preheat to 350°F.
2. Put the ricotta cheese, sugar, orange blossom water, lemon zest, and orange zest in the bowl of a stand mixer fitted with the paddle attachment and paddle at low speed until well blended. (You can also mix in a mixing bowl using a wooden spoon.) Add the eggs one at time, mixing until the mixture is smooth, then fold in the wheat berries until well mixed.

3. Pour the mixture into a pie pan lined with *pasta frolla*. Create a lattice top by arranging three parallel strips at even intervals, then laying three strips over them at a perpendicular angle.

4. Bake until puffed, golden brown, and set but not hard in the center, about 1 hour. Remove the pan from the oven and let cool completely to room temperature before serving.

The pie can be kept in an airtight container at room temperature for 2 to 3 days.

Pasta Frolla

MAKES ONE 10-INCH PIE CRUST WITH LATTICE TOP

In addition to wheat pie, this Italian short dough is used to make a variety of pastries including *pasticiotti* (small custard-filled tarts) and *crostata*. To add a little more flavor, substitute ½ cup almond or pistachio flour for ½ cup of all-purpose flour.

1 cup (2 sticks) unsalted butter, softened
1 cup sugar
½ teaspoon finely grated lemon zest
½ teaspoon pure vanilla extract
½ teaspoon honey, preferably clover
Pinch of baking soda
Pinch of baking powder
¼ cup water
2 cups all-purpose flour

1. Put the butter and sugar in the bowl of stand mixer fitted with the paddle attachment and paddle at medium speed until the butter begins to get fluffy, about 3 minutes. Stop and scrape down the sides of the bowl with a rubber spatula.

2. Add the lemon zest, vanilla, honey, baking soda, and baking powder. Paddle for 1 minute, then stop and scrape.

3. Add the water and paddle at medium speed to work in the water and

BAKING WITH THE CAKE BOSS

create a batter, about 2 minutes. Add the flour and paddle until the dough comes together, about 1 minute, taking care not to overmix.

4. Remove the dough from the bowl, form into a disc, and wrap tightly with plastic wrap. Refrigerate until well chilled, about 30 minutes.

5. Separate out one quarter of the dough and set aside for the lattice topping. Roll out remaining dough to a 14-inch-diameter circle and place in a 10-inch pie pan.

6. Roll out the reserved dough to the same thickness and cut into six ¾-inch strips for a lattice topping.

Apple Pie

MAKES ONE 9-INCH PIE, ENOUGH TO SERVE 10 TO 12

This is a good, old-fashioned American apple pie, with plenty of brown sugar, spices, and a mix of apple varieties to balance the sweet, tangy, and tart flavors. One of my favorite things about this pie is the double crust with the hole in the middle, which gives a little peek at the apples inside. It's easier to make than you might think, although we occasionally have a problem at the bakery that you won't have at home: One of our egg washes has more yolks than the other; the yolkier wash browns much more quickly than the other, and can give the impression that a pie is fully baked even though the filling inside is raw.

3 tablespoons all-purpose flour, plus more for flouring your
    work surface
2 recipes Pie Crust (page 130)
½ cup granulated sugar
½ cup light brown sugar
1 teaspoon ground cinnamon
¼ teaspoon ground ginger
¼ teaspoon ground nutmeg
7 cups thinly sliced, peeled, and cored apples (see Note)
1 tablespoon freshly squeezed lemon juice
2 tablespoons (¼ stick) unsalted butter
1 extra-large egg, beaten

1. Flour your work surface. Roll out one recipe of the dough and line a 9-inch pie pan. Trim off as much overhanging scrap as possible. Refrigerate for at least 1 hour.
2. Position a rack in the center of the oven and preheat to 375°F.
3. Put the 3 tablespoons flour, the granulated sugar, brown sugar, cinnamon, ginger, and nutmeg in a large mixing bowl and mix together by hand.

4. In a separate bowl, toss the apple slices and lemon juice. Sprinkle the sugar mixture over the top and toss to coat the apple pieces.

5. Roll out the remaining pie dough to a 14-inch diameter. Use a cutter or the wide end of a #7 star pastry tip to punch a 1-inch hole in the center of the dough.

6. Put apples in the pie crust and dot the top with pieces of butter. Use a pastry brush to brush the edge of the shell with the beaten egg.

7. Fold the top piece of dough in half so the hole forms a half circle at one edge. Lay the dough over the apples in the pie pan, using the circle as your guide to be sure the top is centered. Unfold the dough and drape it over the rest of the pie. Pat down gently on top. Set the pan on an elevated surface, such as a large can of tomatoes or your turntable, and rotate the pan by hand, using the thumb and fore-finger of one hand to crimp the edges as the pan rotates, creating a trough-like edge. Continue to rotate, pressing the dough against the edge of the pie pan, and the excess will fall off.

8. Paint the top of the pie with the egg wash, painting around but not over the hole.

9. Set the pie in the oven, right on the rack, and bake for 30 minutes, then turn the heat up to 400°F and continue to bake until the top is a deep, burnished golden-brown and the edges have pulled away from the sides a bit and are lightly golden, about 5 more minutes.

10. Remove the pie from the oven and let cool.

Enjoy or cover and store at room temperature for up to 2 days.

Note: Ideally, you would use 1 Red Delicious, 1 Golden Delicious, and 1 Granny Smith. If you use only one type, make it Granny Smith. The most even way to slice apples is on a mandoline.

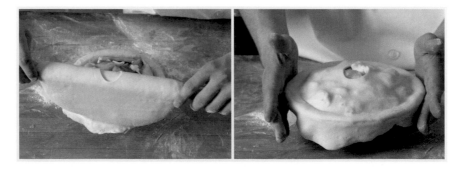

BUDDY VALASTRO

Frutti di Bosco

Italian Fruit Tart

MAKES ONE 9-INCH TART, ENOUGH TO SERVE 10 TO 12

I first had a version of this dessert—a fruit tart made with a butter dough, French cream, and fresh berries—at a New York City restaurant, and liked it so much that I decided I wanted to create our own version of it at Carlo's. It's a perfect summertime dessert because you can use whatever berries you have on hand; raspberries, blueberries, strawberries, blackberries, or a combination would all be right at home here.

In addition to the summertime, we make this during the holidays, when its elegance makes it just right for any gathering from Thanksgiving to New Year's Eve.

1½ cups (3 sticks) unsalted butter
¾ cup granulated sugar
2 extra-large eggs
¼ teaspoon finely grated lemon zest
¼ cup cold water
3 cups pastry flour
1 cup all-purpose flour, plus more for flouring your work surface
1 teaspoon salt
1 teaspoon baking powder
1 cup Italian Custard Cream (page 315)
¾ cup Italian Whipped Cream (page 321)
1 cup blackberries
1 cup blueberries
1 cup raspberries
Powdered (10X) sugar, for serving

1. Position a rack in the center of the oven and preheat to 350°F.
2. Starting on low speed and gradually increasing to medium, cream the butter

and sugar in the bowl of a stand mixer fitted with the paddle attachment. Add the eggs, one at a time, paddling until absorbed into the mixture. Add the zest, then add the water in a thin stream, letting it run down the side of the bowl.

3. Stop the motor and lower the bowl. Put the pastry flour, all-purpose flour, salt, and baking powder in a sifter and sift into the bowl. Starting on low speed and gradually increasing to medium, mix until the dough comes together.

4. Dust your work surface with flour and roll out the dough to a thickness of ⅛ inch. Fit the dough to a 9-inch fluted tart pan. Dock it all over with the tines of a fork.

5. Bake until the dough is lightly golden brown on top and bottom, 15 to 20 minutes. Remove the pan from the oven and let the tart shell cool completely.

6. In a mixing bowl, fold together the custard cream and whipped cream to make French cream.

7. Use a rubber spatula to transfer the French cream to the tart, smoothing the top. Artfully arrange the berries on top. Dust with powdered sugar and serve.

The *frutti di bosco* should be served right away, but can be refrigerated, covered loosely with plastic wrap, for up to 1 day.

Cream Puff Parfait

SERVES 24

My father made this eye-catching dessert for Viennese Hours, the receptions we used to cater at local wedding halls. It's a one-of-a-kind offering that turns cream puffs into the basis of a pyramid-like tower, held together with cream and topped with chocolate shavings, drizzled with melted chocolate, or both. Dad sometimes infused the cream with espresso and scattered espresso beans over the dessert; you can certainly do that. Or experiment with other flavoring agents and finishing touches to personalize this parfait, such as grinding espresso beans and adding them to the cream, which I like to do because adding brewed espresso makes the cream too loose; the longer the cream rests, the more intense the espresso flavor will be.

2 cups heavy cream
½ cup sugar
3 cups Italian Custard Cream (page 315), chilled
2 teaspoons Frangelico, coffee liqueur, Grand Marnier, or Bailey's Irish Cream
24 baked and cooled Cream Puff shells (pages 88, 91)
2 ounces milk chocolate or semisweet chocolate, for shaving over the parfait

1. In a stand mixer fitted with the whip attachment, whip the cream and sugar on medium speed until stiff, about 5 minutes. Transfer the whipped cream to a bowl.
2. Transfer the custard cream to the mixer bowl and whip briefly to smooth out the cream and ensure there are no lumps. Pour in the Frangelico, then slowly add the whipped cream. Stop and scrape the sides and bottom with a rubber spatula, then continue to whip until smooth and airy.
3. Transfer the filling to a pastry bag fitted with the #5 plain tip. Use your pinkie to hollow out the puffs from the bottom and pipe cream into the puffs through the hole. Pipe the cream puffs full of cream.

4. Pipe circles of cream into the bottom of a 9-inch pie pan. Arrange 5 or 6 cream puffs around the circumference of the bottom, and 1 in the center. Build a pyramid of cream puffs, piping cream on top of each layer and around each puff, and smoothing it with a rubber spatula.

5. Refrigerate the parfait at least 4 hours or overnight to set it and allow the flavors to develop. Just before serving, shave the chocolate over the parfait with a box grater.

6. To serve, use two spoons to transfer 1 cream puff to each of 24 plates. Spoon some more cream over the puff and serve.

Finishing Touches

You can also finish the parfait with a drizzle of melted chocolate (melt ¼ cup dark chocolate chips or 2 ounces coarsely chopped chocolate in the top of a double boiler) piped from a parchment pencil (see page 185) and/or with a dusting of cocoa powder.

Cakes and Cupcakes

Long before I had any idea that they would lead to my own television show, cakes were the Promised Land of my baking existence. When you're a young buck just learning the basics of mixing, baking, decorating, and piping, cakes are what you aspire to, what your entire professional arc is directed toward achieving.

For me, cakes felt like a certain kind of destiny because my father, Buddy Sr., was so renowned for his deft touch with a pastry bag, and for his distinct designs. Dad didn't do the kind of theme cakes we're famous for today—nobody did in those days—but he had a remarkable ability to decorate cakes the way a painter paints on canvas. There was an effortlessness, a weightlessness, to his work—buttercream and whipped cream almost seemed to hover above the cake like clouds; chocolate shavings, too, appeared to dance in the air like confetti; and when he wrote on a cake, well, the words popped like a neon sign. You can teach a baker a lot, but at some point either you're born with great hands or you're not. He had them. So do I.

The good news is that you don't have to be born with the hands of a master to achieve success in cake making and decorating. It's like anything else in baking: If you take the time and effort to get good at the component parts, the big picture is easier than you might have ever imagined.

That said, cake making does require you to pass a number of levels before you're ready to really go for it. Before we get to the theme cakes that any *Cake Boss* fan will want to try, I urge you to have a little patience and develop your basic skills, especially the two most important ones: working on a turntable and developing confidence and accuracy with a pastry bag. In fact, before we go any further, I want to explain a little about both of them and how crucial they are to the decorating process.

THE TURNTABLE

The single most important skill you have to develop for icing cakes and cupcakes is learning to synchronize the trio of yourself, a turntable, and a pastry bag. That probably sounds daunting, but it shouldn't. Because as you're about to find out, the turntable does all the work.

If you want to see the value of a turntable, just try to pipe a neat, even circle on the top of a cake, or even around the side. It's all but impossible to pull off, because you'd have to continually change the angle of the pastry bag, and your wrist simply isn't built for that kind of motion and adjustment. When you use a turntable, however, you create a dynamic similar to a machine: your arm stays in one place, the table turns, and the pressure you place on the bag basically deposits cream or icing on the cake in a uniform manner. Your wrist might turn, or your hand might move up and down to create certain effects, sometimes helped by your leaning forward or back, but your arm will always be stationary. That's why you need a good, sturdy, stainless-steel professional-caliber turntable. Because a turntable does so much of the work, you want one that will endure for years of carrying cakes and spinning round and round.

It doesn't matter which way you rotate a turntable; it can go clockwise or counterclockwise and still produce terrific results. As I said up front, at the end of the day, baking and decorating are largely about your individualistic relationship with your tools and ingredients; whichever direction works for you will get the job done. That said, generally speaking, right-handed decorators tend to turn clockwise; lefties counterclockwise. By the way, before being set on a turntable, cakes should be set on a doily on top of a round piece of cardboard the same diameter as the cake.

USING A PASTRY BAG

When you use a pastry bag, you should fill it about two-thirds full, being sure to squeeze the contents as far down into the bag as possible so they can be forced out of the tip with just the slightest pressure.

The proper way to hold a pastry bag is with one hand, resting the weighty, full part of the bag on your forearm and leaning the back of the bag against your upper arm or shoulder for support. This will keep one hand free for turning a turntable or performing other side tasks.

Using a pastry bag effectively is all about pressure. Generally speaking, when you use the bag, you will apply either steady pressure, for creating long lines or piping filling and/or frosting, or a pulsating pressure for creating borders and shapes.

There are four main pressure techniques for working with a pastry bag.

- *Squeeze-and-pull:* Just what it sounds like. This technique involves squeezing and pulling the bag upward to deposit the contents in a dab or blob. The classic example is piping cream puff batter; in cake decorating, we use this technique to create bulbs and dots that punctuate cakes and cupcakes.
- *Steady pressure:* This technique, which involves holding the bag for a sustained period of a few seconds, is used to produce a continuous line or circle of frosting or cream, such as the filling for an éclair or the border on a cupcake.
- *Steady-pressure-and-movement:* This technique involves applying continuous pressure to the bag while moving your hand to create a flourish such as a drop line, a swag, or a loop border. (See page 174 for a loop border.)
- *Pulse:* This technique involves all of the above, squeezing and pulling with pulse and movement—for example, to create a shell border (see page 174, top photo) around the base of a cake.

Decorator's Buttercream

MAKES ABOUT 6 CUPS

Unless otherwise indicated, all of the piping in this section should be executed with decorator's buttercream. To color the cream, mix food coloring in with a rubber spatula until the cream is uniformly colored. Amounts will vary and will be based on the brand of food coloring and how light or dark your want the cream to be. I recommend food-coloring gel, available in small tubes, because it's less watery and easier to work with. Start with a few drops and add more as you mix. If you are making a dark color, like black, the cream can become loose or watery in which case you should mix in some extra powdered sugar until the texture resembles shaving cream. For white decorator's buttercream, or to dirty-ice a cake (Carlo's-speak for applying a crumb coat) before applying fondant, you do not need to add any color.

7½ cups powdered (10X) sugar
2¼ cups vegetable shortening
6 tablespoons (¾ stick) unsalted butter
1½ tablespoons pure vanilla extract
¼ cup plus 2 tablespoons cold water

1. Put the sugar, shortening, butter, and vanilla in the bowl of a stand mixer fitted with the paddle attachment and paddle at low-medium speed until the mixture is smooth, with no lumps, about 3 minutes.
2. With the motor running, add the water in a thin stream and continue to paddle until absorbed, about 3 minutes.

The buttercream can be refrigerated in an airtight container for up to 2 weeks.

How Much Decorator's Buttercream?

In the cake and cupcake decorating instructions that follow, estimated amounts of each color of buttercream required are provided. But no two decorators will use exactly the same amount of buttercream—your roses might be larger or smaller than mine, for example—so don't be worried if you use a bit more or less than is indicated. For most of the cake recipes, the first step is to dirty-ice the cake, which should take approximately 4 cups of buttercream, leaving you 2 cups to color as needed for other purposes such as piping design elements like leaves and grass, and piping a border on the cake. I suggest you dirty-ice the cake before coloring the remaining decorator's buttercream because you can return the icing you scrape off the cake while icing it and making a smooth coating (see page 172) to the bowl with the other uncolored buttercream, which will give you more to work with.

This recipe can be multiplied or divided to produce larger or smaller batches, and leftover buttercream can be refrigerated right in the pastry bag or piped out into another container and refrigerated.

Cupcakes

Believe it or not, the perfect way to practice synchronizing yourself, a pastry bag, and a turntable is by decorating cupcakes. In fact, if you've never worked with a turntable before, I suggest spending a little time decorating cupcakes because—rather than the all-or-nothing prospect of icing and decorating a cake—a batch of cupcakes gives you twenty-four chances to get better, with minimal damage done if you mess one up.

Carlo's flower-themed cupcakes are one of our signature offerings. Created for Mother's Day years ago, they have become so popular that we now offer them all year long. Not only are they visually pleasing and delicious, but they give you a chance to practice your piping skills, specifically, using a turntable and applying the four different types of pressure. The rose cupcake and Christmas tree cupcakes also provide a chance to practice more three-dimensional piping, which helps train you for similar tasks called for in cake decorating.

All of these cupcakes are generally made with Vanilla Cake (page 296) or Chocolate Cake (page 298), although you could also make them with Red Velvet (page 308) or any other of the basic cakes in this book, with the exception of chiffon cakes or sponge cake.

Note that each cupcake calls for at least three different colors/types of buttercream or frosting. When possible, you should have each of them made and in its bag with the proper tip attached before beginning. I have provided estimated amounts called for to make twenty-four of each type of cupcake, but you will probably want to make a variety of types each time you decorate a batch of cupcakes, and you can change the colors as you see fit, so don't be bound by my quantities—try different color combinations to create your own signature cupcakes, making more buttercream and coloring it as needed.

Staying Centered

When working on a turntable, be sure to center the cake or cupcake before going to work on it. If it's not centered, you will end up with a "wobble" effect.

Cupcake Notes

- All cupcakes may be kept in an airtight container at room temperature for up to 3 days.
- Most of these call for only 4 cups of decorator's buttercream; you can refrigerate the remaining 2 cups produced by the recipe, or reduce each ingredient by one-third to produce just 4 cups.
- These cupcakes call for both types of pastry tips: The #126 rose tip is a regular pastry tip (that is, the type that you drop into the bag before the buttercream is added); all others are interchangeable tips that require a coupler. Set up all the pastry bags, icings, and tips before you start.

Sunflower Cupcake

24 cupcakes
1 cup green buttercream, #126 rose tip
2½ cups yellow buttercream, #70 interchangeable leaf tip
½ cup brown buttercream or Chocolate Fudge Frosting (page 313), #133
   interchangeable grass tip

1. Center a cupcake on the turntable.
2. Take the green buttercream bag in hand and, while turning the turntable, apply steady pressure to pipe a border around the edge of the cupcake.
3. Switch to the yellow buttercream bag, and employ the squeeze-and-pull technique to pull leaves from just inside the border (*not* the center of the cupcake) to just over the edge.
4. Switch to the brown buttercream bag and squeeze and pull little strands in the center of the cupcake.
5. Remove the cupcake from the turntable and repeat with the remaining cupcakes.

Note: The colors used for this and the other cupcakes in this section are my suggested colors; feel free to experiment with other colors and combinations to create your own signature look and develop your eye for coordination.

Puff Flower Cupcakes

24 cupcakes
1 cup green buttercream, #126 rose tip
2½ cups pink buttercream, #10 interchangeable plain tip
½ cup orange buttercream, #8 interchangeable plain tip

1. Center a cupcake on the turntable.
2. Take the green buttercream bag in hand and, while turning the turntable, apply steady pressure to pipe a border around the edge of the cupcake.
3. Switch to the pink buttercream bag, and use the squeeze-and-pull technique to form bulbous shell-like petals, pulling in from the inner edge of the green border.
4. Switch to the orange buttercream bag and squeeze-and-pull a dot in the center of the flower.
5. Remove the cupcake from the turntable and repeat with the remaining cupcakes.

Flat-Petal Flower Cupcakes

Unless you have two rose tips, you will need to set up and fill the orange bag after using the green bag. Be sure to clean and dry the tip before dropping it into the bag that will hold the orange buttercream.

24 cupcakes
1 cup green buttercream, #126 rose tip
2½ cups orange buttercream, #126 rose tip
½ cup yellow buttercream, #8 interchangeable plain tip

1. Center a cupcake on the turntable.
2. Take the green buttercream bag in hand and, while turning the turntable, apply steady pressure to pipe a border around the edge of the cupcake.
3. Switch to the orange buttercream bag and apply the steady-pressure-and-movement technique (rotating your wrist) to create wide petals, starting in the center and ending just inside the border.
4. Switch to the yellow buttercream bag and squeeze-and-pull once in the center of the cupcake to make a dot.
5. Remove the cupcake from the turntable and repeat with the remaining cupcakes.

Daisy Cupcakes

24 cupcakes
1 cup green buttercream, #126 rose tip
2½ cups white buttercream, #79 interchangeable lily of the valley tip
½ cup yellow buttercream, #33 interchangeable grass tip

1. Center a cupcake on the turntable.
2. Take the green buttercream bag in hand and, while turning the turntable, apply steady pressure to pipe a border around the edge of the cupcake.
3. Switch to the white buttercream bag and squeeze-and-pull from the center of the cupcake to form petals.
4. Switch to the yellow buttercream bag and finish with a few squeeze-and-pull applications to fill out the center of the flower.
5. Remove the cupcake from the turntable and repeat with the remaining cupcakes.

Buddy's Cabbage Rose Cupcakes

24 cupcakes
1 cup green buttercream, #126 rose tip
5 cups purple buttercream, #104 interchangeable rose tip

1. Center a cupcake on the turntable.
2. Take the green buttercream bag in hand and, while turning the turntable, apply steady pressure to pipe a border around the edge of the cupcake.
3. Switch to the purple buttercream bag and pipe a conical shape in the center of the cupcake. While rotating the turntable, apply steady pressure, turning your wrist to rotate the pastry tip and create a ruffled effect.
4. Remove the cupcake from the turntable and repeat with the remaining cupcakes.

Piping Buttercream Roses

As you can see from the cupcake illustrations, we pipe the flowers directly onto the cupcakes at Carlo's, but you will want to use a rose nail for making roses for both cakes and cupcakes. Piping directly onto cupcakes is best left to the professionals.

1. Take a buttercream bag fitted with the #126 rose tip in your dominant hand and a rose nail in your nondominant hand. Pipe a conical base, 1½ inches high by 1½ inches thick, being sure to release the pressure before lifting the bag from the top of the base.
2. As you rotate the rose nail, hold the bag at a slight angle to the base and apply steady pressure, turning the bag downward to pipe the first rose petal layer, piping all the way around the base.
3. With the bag at a slightly lower angle, pipe three more overlapping petals, but this time pipe only about halfway around the base for each petal.
4. With the bag perpendicular to the rose, pipe five more overlapping petals,

wider this time, and piping only about one third of the way around the rose for each petal.

5. Finish by piping five more overlapping layers just under the five piped in step 4.

6. To transfer a rose to a cupcake or cake, put down the pastry bag and pick up a pair of scissors. Open the shears and very gently close them under the rose. Lift the rose off the nail and deposit it in the desired location on the cake, using the edge of the rose nail to gently pull the rose off the scissors.

Red Rose Cupcakes

Unless you have two rose tips, you will need to set up and fill the red bag after using the green bag. Be sure to clean and dry the tip before dropping it into the bag that will hold the red buttercream.

24 cupcakes
1 cup green buttercream, #126 rose tip
5 cups red buttercream, #126 rose tip

1. Center a cupcake on the turntable.
2. Take the green buttercream bag in hand and, while turning the turntable, apply steady pressure to pipe a border around the edge of the cupcake.
3. Switch to the red buttercream bag, pipe a rose, and transfer it to the top of the cupcake. (For more, see "Piping Buttercream Roses," page 164.)
4. Remove the cupcake from the turntable and repeat with the remaining cupcakes.

Christmas Tree Cupcakes

24 CUPCAKES

1 cup green buttercream, in a bag fitted with the #126 rose tip
5½ cups green buttercream, in a bag set up for an interchangeable tip
½ cup red buttercream, #2 interchangeable plain tip
½ cup yellow buttercream, #3 interchangeable plain tip
¼ cup nonpareils
½ cup white buttercream in a parchment pencil (see page 185)

1. Center a cupcake on the turntable.
2. Take the first green buttercream bag in hand and, while turning the turn-table, apply steady pressure to pipe a border around the edge of the cupcake.
3. Attach a #12 plain tip to the coupler of the second bag of green buttercream and pipe a 2-inch-high cylinder. (If you have another color of icing already bagged, you can pipe the cylinder with another color, like white, as pictured. The cylinder will be covered by the leaves, so its color doesn't matter.)
4. Replace the #12 plain tip with the #69 leaf tip and squeeze-and-pull green leaves all over the cylinder.
5. Switch to the red buttercream bag, and squeeze-and-pull small dots all over the tree, representing ornaments.

6. Switch to the yellow buttercream bag, and squeeze-and-pull a "star" (a small "kiss"-like accent) on the top of the tree.

7. Sprinkle nonpareils over the tree. If desired, top each tree with a sugar star, as pictured.

8. Take the parchment pencil in hand and apply steady pressure to pipe 2 strands of white "glitter" in the branches of the tree.

9. Remove the cupcake from the turntable and repeat with the remaining cupcakes.

Note: These cupcakes call for about 8 cups, or 1½ batches, of Decorator's Buttercream.

Working with Cakes

Okay, now it's time to begin working with cakes. In this section, I'll show you how to make the natural progression from trimming and icing cakes to piping techniques to the basics of fondant, and then some home versions of the *Cake Boss*–style cakes we make on the show.

The basic cake recipes are found starting on page 295, and basic frostings and fillings on page 311.

TRIMMING AND CUTTING CAKES

Whether you're working with icing or fondant, the first step in decorating any cake is trimming and cutting it. Use a serrated knife to remove the top layer of discolored "skin" of browned cake to make a flat top. Because it makes the cake easier to cut evenly, I like to work with a frozen cake. Now, freezing sometimes gets a bad rap in the food world because people associate it with TV dinners and frozen pizzas. But there are times when a freezer can be your best friend. I don't insist on it in the recipes, but freezing a freshly baked and cooled cake is one of the best things you can do. It seals in all the moisture, whereas cakes tend to dry out in the refrigerator. Also, if you plan to ice and/or decorate a cake, it will be firmer when it emerges from the freezer, and you'll have an easier time trimming, halving, and icing it.

Cakes should be frozen for 1 to 2 hours for optimum trimming texture. You can freeze them for longer, but they will become very hard and should be allowed to thaw slightly before you try to cut into them. Do not try to trim a cake that's

hard as a rock because the knife can slip, very dangerously. Be sure the cake has a little give to it before you start trimming.

If the cake you're making requires you to cut it in half horizontally, first set it on your turntable or work surface. Kneel or bend so that the cake is at eye level and you can get a good head-on look at it. Keep your eye fixed on the point where the knife enters the cake and as you apply pressure to the top with your free hand, rotate the cake against the knife, keeping it straight to get a nice, even cut. If you will be filling a cake, always try to make the layers level with each other, trimming if necessary so they will rest straight when stacked.

FILLING AND ICING CAKES

I like to use a pastry bag to fill cakes because it's the right tool no matter what filling or frosting you are using—it reduces the amount of spreading and scraping required to neatly fill and ice a cake. If you're using a thick cream for a filling, then using a spatula might cause the cake to break. Similarly, a soaked sponge cake will come apart if you spend too much time working on it with a spatula.

Filling Cakes

To fill a cake using a pastry bag, fit the bag with the #6 plain tip. Set the first layer of cake on the turntable. Apply steady pressure (see page 153) to pipe the filling in concentric circles, stopping to lift the bag after completing each circle. After the layer is covered with frosting circles, use your cake icing spatula to gently smooth it out into an even layer. Carefully set the next layer on top, gently pressing down to ensure it's nice and level. Then lay down the next layer of filling in the same manner.

Icing (Frosting) Cakes

Before icing a cake, double-check to be sure the layers look nice and straight and aligned, and be sure the cake is centered on your turntable. Even a four-layer cake should have the same shape as an uncut cake. If necessary, trim the layers to level them, or use a little extra icing under uneven layers to straighten them.

Put the frosting in a pastry bag fitted with a #6 or #7 star tip. You can use either tip for icing a cake; the #7 will give a slightly larger piping effect. For dirty-icing with decorator's buttercream, described on page 197, the #6 tip is the more logical choice.

Spinning the turntable, apply steady pressure to the bag to pipe concentric circles on top of the cake, stopping and lifting the bag between circles. Then, also spinning the table, pipe frosting around the sides, starting at the top and working your way down.

Use the cake icing spatula to smooth the circles on top of the cake together, by holding the spatula parallel to the cake top, and spinning the turntable, gradually lowering the surface of the spatula close to the cake. Turn your spatula perpendicular to the cake and smooth the sides, again

---

Ratios of Filling to Cake

The appropriate balance of flavors and textures varies from cake to cake, but there are some guidelines that apply most of the time.

Chocolate Ganache (page 318), Italian Buttercream (page 314), Vanilla Frosting (page 312), Chocolate Fudge Frosting (page 313), and Cream Cheese Frosting (page 316) are all rather dense and rich, so the proper ratio of filling to cake is 1:2, meaning a layer of filling should be approximately half the height of a layer of cake.

Italian Custard Cream (page 315), Cannoli Cream (page 109), Italian Whipped Cream (page 321), Lobster Tail Cream (page 320), and My Dad's Chocolate Mousse (page 317) are relatively airy and do not threaten to overwhelm the flavor or texture of the cake, so the proper ratio of filling to cake is 1:1, meaning a layer of filling should be approximately the same height as a layer of cake.

BUDDY VALASTRO

gradually moving the spatula closer to the cake. (Note that a decorator's comb was used to produce the ridges on the side of the cake pictured; for instructions on using a decorator's comb, see page 184.)

Finally, while spinning the turntable, hold the spatula parallel to the top of the cake and lower it just to smooth the top one last time to level it off and ready it for decorating.

SOAKING A SPONGE CAKE

As their name suggests, Italian sponge cakes (see page 304) are made to be soaked with Syrup (see page 322). You might snack on a vanilla, chocolate, or carrot cake with no frosting, but you wouldn't do the same with a sponge cake because it's dense and dry until it's been soaked.

To soak a sponge cake, use a pastry brush to generously apply the syrup to the cake, pausing periodically to let the cake soak it up. You might be surprised how much syrup a cake can take on.

In layering a sponge cake, do not apply the syrup to the layers until they are on the cake; they will break if you try to lift them after soaking.

A sponge cake will deepen in flavor during a day or two in the refrigerator. Store on a plate, covered loosely with plastic wrap.

DECORATING TECHNIQUES

There's no limit to what designs and patterns you can make on a cake, but here are some of the techniques we use most often at Carlo's Bake Shop. If you've never worked with a pastry bag, fondant, or modeling chocolate before, you should be prepared for a period of growth and development, but most people find that they improve quickly. Just be patient, and remember what my father always said: "There's nothing in decorating that you can't fix."

BASIC PIPING TECHNIQUES

On iced cakes, I like to apply a border to both the top and the bottom. Top borders can make a cake look bigger or smaller: If the border is piped inside the edge of the cake, it makes the cake look *smaller*. If the border is piped outside the edge of the cake, it makes the cake look *larger*. My favorite border for the bottom of a cake is a shell border (see next page).

A shell border can be made with a number of different regular or interchangeable tips, and in just about any size or shape.

To pipe a shell border (at left), position the tip at the bottom of the cake. Squeeze and pull as you slowly rotate the turntable. Continue all the way around until you return to the starting point.

Other Borders:

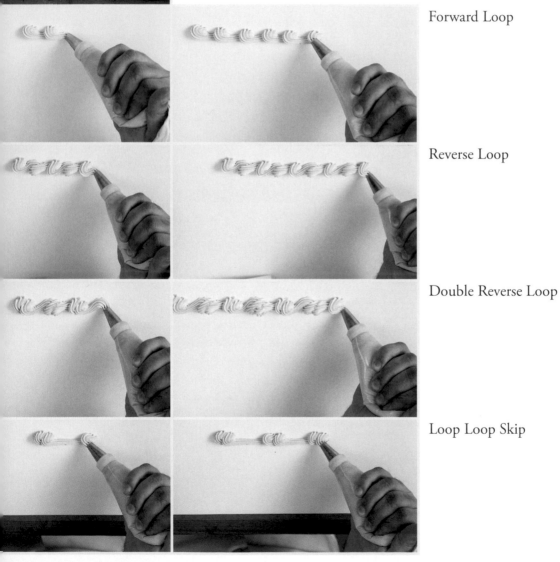

Forward Loop

Reverse Loop

Double Reverse Loop

Loop Loop Skip

Shell

Rope

Dot

"S"

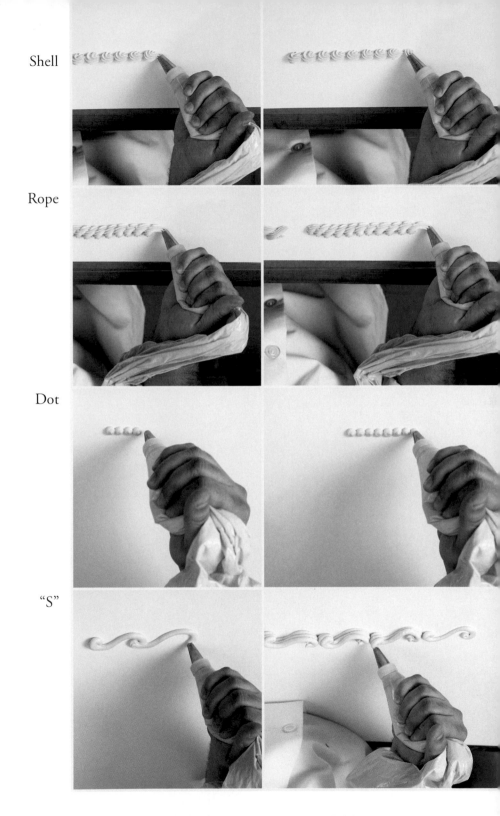

Forward Loop

Reverse Loop

Double Reverse Loop

Loop Loop Skip

Shell

Rope

Dot

"S"

Leaf

DECORATION FOR SIDES OF THE CAKE

Swags

Use a small interchangeable tip, such as #103. Apply steady pressure and an up-and-down motion with your wrist. Move only the wrist/hand; the arm stays still.

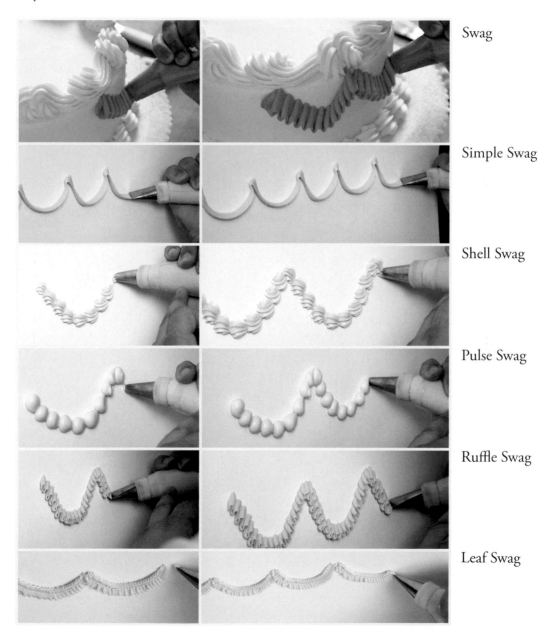

Swag

Simple Swag

Shell Swag

Pulse Swag

Ruffle Swag

Leaf Swag

Drop Lines

For drop lines you need perfectly smooth buttercream with no air in it; it should be fluffy and smooth as shaving cream. Use a #2, #3, or #4 plain interchangeable tip.

Keep your arm still and lean away as you turn the table.

Let the line drop, then . . .

. . . lean forward and place the other end of the line on the cake.

Release.

Repeat until you return to the starting point.

To make a double drop line repeat the same steps, making slightly shorter drop lines just above the first lines, but ending each drop line at the same point. You can make variations by adding intersecting drop lines.

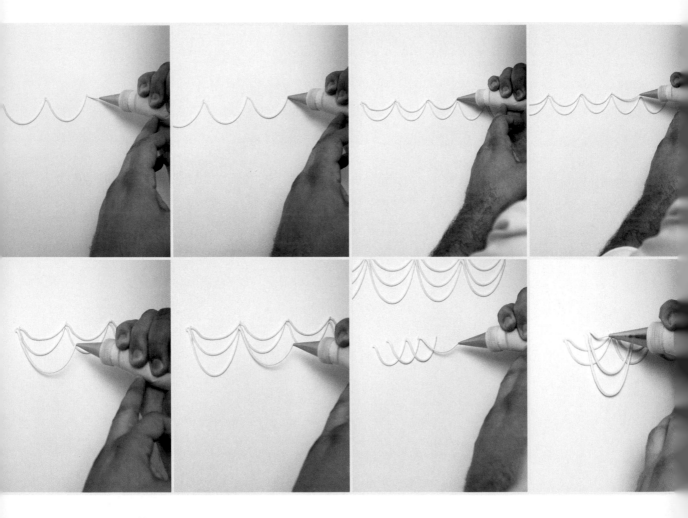

Filigree Piping

I call filigree piping "drawing on the cake." Generally speaking, you want to use a #2 or #3 plain tip. Filigree piping is freestyle piping, but the rule of thumb is to keep the individual design elements from touching each other. Here are some of my favorite filigree patterns.

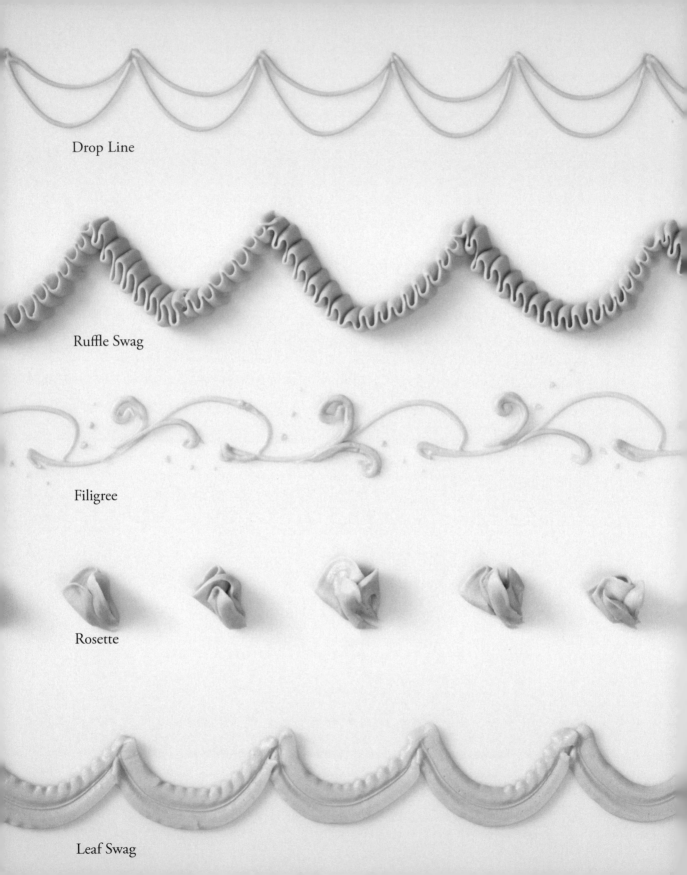

Drop Line

Ruffle Swag

Filigree

Rosette

Leaf Swag

Other Design Possibilities:

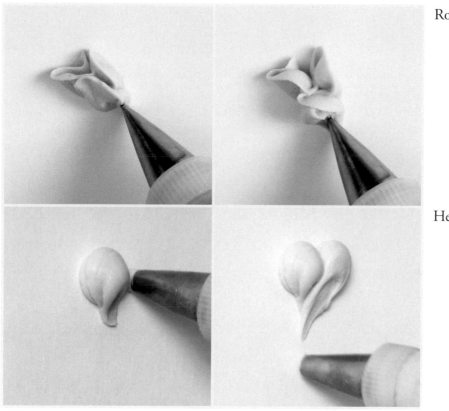

Rosette

Heart

Children's Birthday Cakes

Classic birthday cakes are something every baker should be able to make. They offer a chance to put many of the basic cake decorating skills just described to use.

A Boy's Birthday Cake

EDIBLES

Two 9-inch cakes, and your choice of filling

6 cups white Decorator's Buttercream (page 154) in a pastry bag
fitted with the #6 star tip

1½ cups blue buttercream in a pastry bag fitted with the #126 rose
tip

½ cup green buttercream in a pastry bag fitted with the #67
interchangeable leaf tip

½ cup blue buttercream in a parchment pencil (page 185)

TOOLS AND EQUIPMENT

Decorator's comb (optional)

1. Prepare the cake: Prepare a double-layer cake on a doily-lined card-board circle, filling it with the filling of your choice, and icing it with white buttercream. If you have a decorator's comb, use it to create a ridged effect along the side of the cake (see "Decorator's Comb," page 184).

2. Pipe a border around the base: Pipe a large shell border around the bottom of the cake by rotating the turntable and pulsing the white decorator's buttercream bag.

3. Pipe a border around the top: Use the same bag to pipe a single reverse shell border (aka Figure 8 Loop) on top of the cake.

4. Pipe buds: Take the blue buttercream bag in hand and pipe buds between every other loop of the top border, squeezing as you rotate your wrist. Pipe buds along the shell border at the bottom of the cake, aligning them between every other bud at the top of the cake.

5. Make buttercream roses: Make 3 blue buttercream roses (see page 164) and apply them to the back of the cake (see "Face Front," page 186), angling them toward the front by piping a dab of blue but-tercream underneath.

6. Add leaves to the flowers: Take the green buttercream bag in hand

and squeeze-and-pull leaves onto the cake, beginning under the edge of the flowers and pulling outward. Pipe smaller leaves between the flowers.

7. Write Happy Birthday: Use the parchment pencil to write Happy Birthday, holding the pencil at an angle and writing with continuous pressure. (For more, see "To write with a parchment pencil," page 186.)

8. For an optional finishing touch: Use the parchment pencil to further decorate the cake with little blue dots.

Decorator's Comb

A decorator's comb, also sometimes called a "triangle," can be used to add ridges to the side of a cake. Hold the comb flush against the cake, with the bottom edge against the turntable, and rotate the turntable.

Make Your Own Parchment Pencil

If you don't have a pastry bag on hand, or if all of your bags are filled with colors you aren't using, you can fashion a quick parchment pencil for small jobs such as writing on cakes, drizzling molten chocolate, or fashioning small leaves.

To make a parchment pencil:

1. Make a parchment triangle: Cut a 12-inch square piece of parchment paper diagonally in half, either with scissors or by laying it on a cutting board or work surface and slicing through it with the tip of a very sharp knife, to create two triangles. You will use only one triangle; save the other for the next time you need a parchment pencil.
2. Make a parchment cone: With one hand, hold the triangle in front of you with the point facing down. Use your other hand to wrap the paper around itself into a cone, coming around twice to use up all the paper.
3. Tighten the cone: Pinch the wide, open end of the cone with your thumb and forefinger and rub your fingers together repeatedly to tighten the cone. It should still be wide at the open end and tightened into a firm, conical shape.
4. Fill the cone: Use a tablespoon or small rubber spatula to fill the cone about two thirds with buttercream icing or melted chocolate. Hold the cone securely so it doesn't unravel and the tip doesn't become wider than you want it.

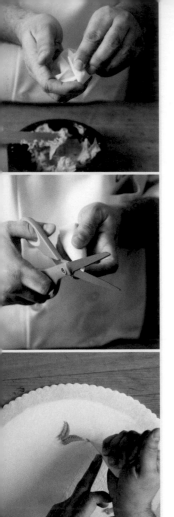

5. Close the open end: Roll the open end closed over the buttercream, pressing down to pack the cream in tightly all the way to the tip.
6. Cut the tip: Use scissors to snip off the tip of the cone and approximate the effect of a pastry tip. For a plain tip, cut as far up as you need to for the width you desire. For a leaf tip, flatten out the tip by pressing on it and cut a "V" shape.

Note: The parchment pencil can be kept at room temperature for up to 2 days.

To write with a parchment pencil:

Hold the pencil at a 45-degree angle, slightly above the cake, and applying continuous pressure, let icing drop onto the cake as you write. If you cannot maintain continuous pressure for the length of time it takes to write a word, stop after a letter, flex your hand, then continue.

To make leaves with a parchment pencil:

Cut a "V" at the narrow end of the cone. To pipe leaves, employ the squeeze-and-pull technique, making the leaves wider at the back and tapering toward the front. *Tip:* Put the middle finger of your nondominant hand about 1 inch up from the point of the pencil for support and guidance.

Face Front

There's always a front and a back to a cake. Unless you are trying to divert attention from an imperfection, it doesn't matter which side is the front, but it's important to establish it so that everything flows in the same direction. For example, when you put flowers down, you want to tilt them toward the front.

BUDDY VALASTRO

A Girl's Birthday Cake

Two 9-inch cakes, filled with your choice of filling
6 cups white Decorator's Buttercream (page 154) in a pastry bag
fitted with the #6 star tip
1½ cups pink buttercream in a pastry bag fitted with the #126
rose tip
½ cup pink buttercream in a parchment pencil (see page 185)
1 cup white buttercream in a pastry bag fitted with the #6 plain
interchangeable tip
½ cup green buttercream in a pastry bag fitted with the #67 inter-
changeable leaf tip

1. Prepare the cake: Prepare a double-layer cake on a doily-lined card-board circle, filling it with the filling of your choice, and icing it with white decorator's buttercream, using the bag fitted with the star tip.
2. Pipe a border around the base: Pipe a large shell border around the bottom of the cake by rotating the turntable and applying pulse pressure to the same white buttercream bag.
3. Pipe a border around the top: Still using the same white buttercream bag, pipe a double loop border just inside the edge on top of the cake.
4. Add swags to the side of the cake: Switch to the pink buttercream bag and make swags from the top of the cake about halfway down the side, applying continuous pressure and a wavy motion, turning your hand up and down at the wrist, but keeping your arm still.
5. Pipe a border on top of the cake: Use the parchment pencil to pipe a border just inside the edge of the cake. Angle the pencil toward the cake and squeeze, rotating the turntable and moving your hand to create the design of the frame.
6. Pipe circles where swags meet the top of the cake: Use the white buttercream bag with the #6 plain interchangeable tip to pipe over-lapping circles (two or three on top of each other) where the swags meet the top edge of the cake.

7. Make buttercream roses: Use the pink buttercream bag to make three flowers (see page 164) on a rose nail. Make each flower slightly smaller than the previous one. Contour the flowers along the inner edge of the cake and angle each one upward by piping a dab of buttercream under each one before setting it down.

8. Add leaves to the flowers: Take the green buttercream bag in hand and squeeze leaves onto the cake, beginning under the edge of the flowers and pulling outward. Pipe smaller leaves between the flowers.

9. Write "Happy Birthday": Use the parchment pencil to write Happy Birthday to the left of the flowers, letting the pink border frame the words.

Create Your Own Cakes

The two birthday cakes should give you a solid, basic foundation in the techniques called for to fill, ice, and decorate. Using the recipes at the end of this chapter as a guide, you should feel free to experiment with different combinations and designs. To get you started, here's a chart of possible combinations that you can use to produce some of the cakes we've made at Carlo's over the years.

MY FAVORITE CAKE COMBINATIONS

Here are my favorite combinations of cakes, fillings, and frostings, with tips on how to make them.

Vanilla Cake Combinations
(For Vanilla Cake recipe, see page 296)

NAME	LAYERS	FILLING	RATIO*	FROSTING	OTHER FLOURISHES**
Raspberry Dream Cake	3	Lobster Tail Cream (page 320) topped with fresh raspberries	1:2	Italian Whipped Cream (page 321)	Each cake layer is half of a 9-inch cake; save extra half cake for another use, or crumble by hand and apply crumbs to sides of cake.
Notes: Between bottom layer and middle layer, and middle layer and top layer, apply a layer of lobster tail cream and arrange raspberries on top in concentric circles starting from the center and working out.					
The Oklahoma	2	Chocolate Fudge (page 313)	1:2	Chocolate Fudge (page 313)	
Notes: Each layer is a full 9-inch cake. Be sure to double the frosting recipe because you are using it as both filling and frosting.					
Strawberry Shortcake	3	Italian Whipped Cream (page 321) topped with fresh strawberries	1:1	Italian Whipped Cream (page 321)	I don't like mint on my strawberry short-cake, but if you do, by all means scatter chopped mint over this cake.
Notes: Be sure to double the whipped cream recipe because you are using it as both filling and frosting. Thinly slice the strawberries and arrange them over the whipped cream on each layer.					
The Continental	4	My Dad's Chocolate Mousse (page 317) and Chocolate Ganache (page 318)	1:1	My Dad's Chocolate Mousse (page 317) and Chocolate Ganache (page 318)	
Notes: Double the recipes for both mousse and ganache. Put a thick layer (equal to the height of one cake layer) of mousse between cake layers. Ice with mousse and finish by pouring warm ganache over the top.					

*Ratio is filling to cake height.

**If no specific flourish is suggested, I encourage you to use your imagination and the techniques you've learned to create your own uniquely styled cakes.

Chocolate Cake Combinations
(For Chocolate Cake recipe, see page 298)

NAME	LAYERS	FILLING	RATIO*	FROSTING	OTHER FLOURISHES**
Chocolate Mousse Cake	3	My Dad's Chocolate Mousse (page 317), Chocolate Ganache (page 318), and fresh raspberries	1:1	My Dad's Chocolate Mousse (page 317)	Cut extra half cake into eight triangles, shaped like pizza slices. Pipe small rosettes of mousse in 8 spots along perimeter of top, and arrange triangles on an angle, leaning them on the mousse.

Notes: Double the mousse recipe. For the filling, first apply the mousse, then a layer of fresh raspberries, then a thin layer of poured ganache.

Chocolate Fudge Cake	2	Chocolate Fudge (page 313)	1:2	Vanilla (page 312)	

Notes: Double the frosting recipe.

Vanilla Devil's Food Cake	2	Vanilla Frosting (page 312)	1:2	Chocolate Fudge (page 313)	

Notes: Double the frosting recipe.

Buddy Delight	2	Italian Whipped Cream (page 321), fresh strawberries and bananas, Chocolate Ganache (page 318)	1:1	Italian Whipped Cream (page 321)	If desired, finish with chocolate shavings.

Notes: Double the whipped cream recipe. To assemble the cake, top the bottom layer with whipped cream, then with thin slices of banana and strawberry, and pour a thin layer of ganache on top. Top with the remaining cake, then ice with whipped cream.

Lisa's Dream Cake	3	Lobster Tail Cream (page 320) and fresh strawberries	1:1	Italian Whipped Cream (page 321)	Each cake layer is half of a 9-inch cake; save extra half cake for another use, or crumble by hand and apply crumbs to sides of cake.

Notes: For each layer of filling, apply a layer of lobster tail cream, then top by arranging strawberry slices in concentric circles starting from the center and working out.

*Ratio is filling to cake height.

**If no specific flourish is suggested, I encourage you to use your imagination and the techniques you've learned to create your own uniquely styled cakes.

Italian Sponge Cake Combinations
(For Italian Sponge Cake recipe, see page 304)

NAME	LAYERS	FILLING	RATIO*	FROSTING	OTHER FLOURISHES**
Old-Fashioned Italian Rum Cake	2 (from 1 cake)	Rum Syrup (page 322), Italian Custard Cream (page 315), and fresh strawberries	1:1	Italian Whipped Cream (page 321)	
		Notes: Halve cake horizontally. Soak bottom half with syrup and top with custard cream, then sliced fresh strawberries. Top with the other cake half, soak top half with syrup, and ice with whipped cream.			
Traditional Italian Wedding Cake	3 (from 1½ cakes)	Rum Syrup (page 322), Italian Custard Cream (page 315), Chocolate Custard Cream (page 315)	1:1	Italian Whipped Cream (page 321)	Garnish on the sides with toasted slivered almonds, if desired.
		Notes: Halve cakes horizontally. Soak bottom layer with syrup, and top with custard cream. Set another layer on top, soak with syrup, and top with chocolate custard cream. Top with final layer, soak with syrup, then ice cake with whipped cream.			
New Age Cassata Cake	2 (from 1 cake)	Strega Syrup (page 322), Cannoli Cream (page 109)	1:1	Italian Whipped Cream (page 321)	Garnish on the sides with toasted slivered almonds, if desired.
		Notes: Halve cake horizontally.			

*Ratio is filling to cake height.

**If no specific flourish is suggested, I encourage you to use your imagination and the techniques you've learned to create your own uniquely styled cakes.

Other Cake Combinations

NAME	LAYERS	FILLING	RATIO*	FROSTING	OTHER FLOURISHES**
Strawberry Chiffon (Make with **White Chiffon cake,** page 300)	2 (from 1 cake)	Italian Whipped Cream (page 321) and fresh strawberries	1:1	None	
	Notes: Fill the cake with the whipped cream and sliced fresh strawberries, and ice it with the same. Then garnish with fresh strawberries on top.				
Lemon Chiffon (Make with **White Chiffon cake,** page 300)	2	Lemon Cream	1:1	None	Dust finished cakes with powdered (10X) sugar, if desired.
	Notes: Cut each cake in thirds. Make a lemon cream by folding together 1 recipe Italian Whipped Cream (page 321) and 1 recipe Italian Custard Cream (page 315) and adding the juice and finely grated zest of 2 large lemons. Ice the cakes between the layers with the cream.				
Chocolate Chiffon (Make with **Chocolate Chiffon cake,** page 302)	2 (from 1 cake)	My Dad's Chocolate Mousse (page 317), fresh strawberries, Chocolate Ganache (page 318)	1:1	My Dad's Chocolate Mousse (page 317)	Dust finished cakes with powdered (10X) sugar, if desired.
	Notes: Fill with mousse and berries, then a thin layer of ganache. Ice with mousse. Pipe six rosettes of mousse on top, and set a giant strawberry between each of the rosettes, then drizzle the cake with ganache.				
Red Velvet Cake (Make with **Red Velvet cake,** page 308)	2	Cream Cheese (page 316)	1:2	Cream Cheese (page 316)	
	Notes: Fill the cake with cream cheese frosting and ice with the same.				
Carrot Cake (Make with **Carrot cake,** page 306)	2	Cream Cheese (page 316)	1:2	Cream Cheese (page 316)	
	Notes: Fill the cake with cream cheese frosting and ice with the same.				

*Ratio is filling to cake height.

**If no specific flourish is suggested, I encourage you to use your imagination and the techniques you've learned to create your own uniquely styled cakes.

Fondant

Fondant is a sugar dough that can be purchased in different colors. Because you usually see it only on professionally decorated cakes, most people assume that it is difficult to work with, but the truth is that for many home bakers and decorators, I dare say it will be easier to manipulate than frosting and buttercream. I strongly recommend Satin Ice brand fondant because its colors are especially vibrant and its texture is always consistent.

There's a lot to recommend fondant: You don't have to mix it yourself, it can be held at room temperature, and you can simply cut shapes from it to make designs—an infinitely easier process than developing that elusive Hand of the Bag.

If you have kids, fondant is also a great way to involve them in decorating because they can cut shapes, even using cookie cutters, which give them a greater chance for success.

FONDANT TOOLS

There's almost no end to the tools you can use to make fondant cakes, and a number of the cakes that follow call for specific cutters and implements. But a good basic set of tools for working with fondant includes the following.

- Water pen: This professional tool allows you to apply dabs of water that act as glue with fondant. (If you don't have one, in most cases—except when working with very small pieces—you can use a pastry brush to apply water.)
- Pizza cutter and/or sharp, thin-bladed knife, such as an X-Acto or paring knife: For trimming fondant and cutting shapes
- Strip cutter set: Essential for cutting strips of various sizes from fondant
- Smoother: This iron-shaped device is used to smooth the top of fondant-draped cakes.
- Ruler: For precision
- Paint brush: For applying petal dust
- Steamer: To finish any fondant design, you can steam the fondant in order to evaporate the cornstarch (or powdered sugar) and give it a smooth, shiny look. You can do this with a fabric steamer, or even an inexpensive travel iron. Pass the steamer 1 or 2 inches over the cake, gently waving it to distribute the steam, until the fondant glistens slightly with moisture. Let the fondant air-dry; this should take only a

few seconds. Be careful not to let the steamer spit or spray water onto the cake.

STORING FONDANT

Keep fondant in the airtight container it comes in, at room temperature, until you use it. After removing the portion you plan to work with, store the remaining fondant, if any, in an airtight plastic bag in the tub at room temperature.

WORKING WITH FONDANT

Working with fondant is easier than it might seem. Once you get over the initial "newness" of the medium, you might even find it easier than working with buttercream. Here are the basics of getting started with fondant.

- Wash your work surface. Fondant is a magnet for anything and everything—crumbs, debris, or anything else on your work surface will become embedded in the fondant. Even if you manage to get these particles out, they will leave little divots in the surface that cannot be patched over cleanly. So before beginning, brush your surface, wipe it down with a damp cloth, then dry it thoroughly.
- Before working with fondant, knead it for 1 minute to loosen it and activate the gums.

COATING A CAKE WITH FONDANT

This is the step that all fondant cakes have in common, and it's actually a series of small steps.

DIRTY-ICE THE CAKE

The first step that must be taken is to "dirty-ice" the cake, readying it to receive the fondant. "Dirty-icing" is Carlo's Bake Shop–speak for what most bakers call a "crumb coat." It refers to a thin layer of Decorator's Buttercream (page 154) that's laid down as a frosting to help fondant "stick" to the cake. (It might be helpful to think of it as a primer coat of paint.) The proper name, "crumb coat," refers to the fact that you can see crumbs through the icing. It's not important that your dirty-icing be perfect, just that it be thin and cover the entire cake.

To dirty-ice a cake, first ice it as you usually would; see "Icing (Frosting) Cakes," page 172. Then use a piece of poster board to finish the job (see "Icing with Cardboard," page 198), getting as close to the cake as possible.

After dirty-icing a cake, refrigerate it until the buttercream stiffens, 30 to 60 minutes.

Saving Bags

Many of the theme cakes in this book call for white (uncolored) decorator's buttercream to be used both dirty-icing the cake and for piping some design elements, usually with an interchangeable tip. To avoid using two different bags—one fitted with the #6 star tip for dirty-icing, the other with an interchangeable tip—pipe the buttercream for dirty-icing with a bag fitted with the coupler, but no tip, then attach the interchangeable tip called for in the decorating instructions. This alternative is noted in directions for the cakes to which it applies.

Icing with Cardboard

If you don't have a cake icing spatula on hand, you can do a very clean job using a piece of poster board. In fact, when you dirty-ice a cake prior to working with fondant, finishing the job with a piece of poster board is essential.

To do this, cut a 4 by 3-inch piece of poster board with very sharp scissors. As you rotate the turntable, hold the edge of the cardboard flush against the edge of the cake. Then turn your attention to the top of the cake, combing in with brushstrokes from the edge of the cake, only halfway across at first, then all the way across. Professional decorators actually prefer this technique because it puts your hands in closer contact with the cake itself, giving you greater control than with a spatula, although less seasoned decorators will probably have greater success icing their cakes in two steps—first using a cake icing spatula, then finishing with the poster board.

ROLL OUT THE FONDANT

This is one of the most important steps in working with fondant. As proud as we are of our rolling skills, at Carlo's we use a sheeter to roll out our fondant. At home, you can get a good result working by hand, but it takes some practice and focus.

1. Dust your work surface with cornstarch or powdered (10X) sugar. Some people use flour, which is a fine alternative, but cornstarch is smoother and lighter, and easier to brush or steam off when you're finished.

2. Remove the fondant required from its storage bag/tub. To coat a two-layer, 9-inch cake—which is what most of the cakes in this chapter are—begin with a 3-pound piece. This will be more than you need, but the excess can be returned to the storage bag.

3. Knead the fondant for about 1 minute to activate the gums and make it pliable. If you're working in cold weather, wash your hands in warm water before beginning; warm hands make this job go faster. Just be sure to dry them thoroughly before starting to knead.

4. Dust your work surface with more cornstarch; do this as often as necessary when you work to keep the fondant from pulling or sticking.

5. Flatten out the ball of fondant with the palm of your hand. Begin rolling it, preferably with a polyurethane rolling pin (second choice would be a sturdy, ball-bearing rolling pin), really putting your forearms and weight into the rolling motion. The trick here is to lift the fondant up off the work surface frequently to keep it from sticking; cornstarch helps here, but you need to strike a delicate balance: too much cornstarch will cause the fondant to dry out by drawing out

its moisture. The heat from your hands helps with this. Get into the habit of rubbing the fondant constantly to keep it from drying out.

6. Once you have rolled the fondant out to a length of 18 inches, turn the piece horizontally and fluff it, moving it around to pick up excess cornstarch from the work surface on the bottom. Then roll the other way. As the fondant begins to take on a circular shape, vary the angle of your rolling, first in one direction, then the other. Continue in this fashion until you have rolled a near-perfect circle, 20 to 22 inches in diameter and ⅛ inch thick, or thinner if you're able. The more you turn the fondant, the thinner and more uniform the result will be.

7. Check the fondant for air pockets (bubbles), poking with a needle tool, or a toothpick. After doing this, smooth out the fondant by hand or with a smoother.

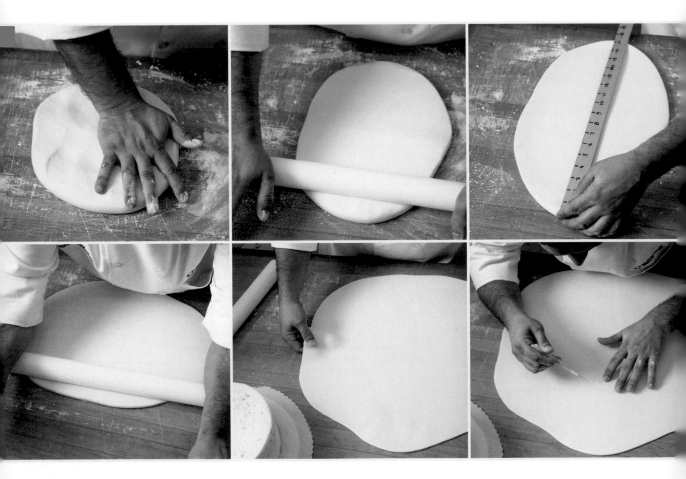

APPLY THE FONDANT TO THE CAKE

1. Set the rolling pin at the far edge of the fondant circle and roll it back toward you, spooling the fondant up onto the pin and gently knocking off any excess cornstarch.

2. Bring the pin over the cake, unspooling the fondant and lowering it over the other side, letting it drape over the sides and onto your work surface Smooth the top with a smoother, then pull and press down gently on the sides to make the fondant taut all around.

3. Caress the fondant with your hands to smooth it against the cake, stretching and pulling it tautly over the top and down the sides, turning the cake and using your fingers to be sure it's smooth all over.

4. Use a pizza cutter or sharp, thin-bladed knife such as a paring knife, to cut around the base and remove any excess fondant. Lift the excess

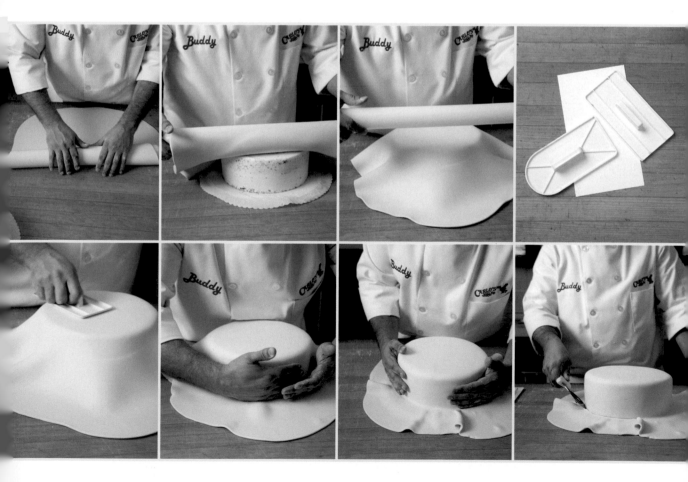

ring up and over the cake. Ball up the excess fondant and return it to its storage bag; it can be reused.

5. Put the cake on a turntable. Use a smoother to smooth out the fondant on the top and sides. Inspect the cake; if you find any dry spots (they will appear arid and veined), rub a little vegetable shortening over them, then smooth with the smoother.

You are now ready to decorate your cake!

Note: Most of the cakes in this book mask the edge where the fondant ends with a piped-on shell border. If designing your own cakes, you can select your own border type, or cut a strip of fondant in another color and make a band. Pipe a thin line of buttercream around the bottom of the cake and wrap the band around it; the cream will cause the fondant to adhere to the cake.

MAKING FONDANT CAKES

Ready to make a few fondant cakes? Before we begin, a few notes:

- The choice of cake and fillings for the following cakes is entirely up to you. Most are best made with vanilla or chocolate cake, but you can try them with other types of cake, such as red velvet or carrot cake.
- The colors of fondant called for in these cakes are all available from

Satin Ice, and the names I use track their product names. (In a few cases you will have to knead two premade colors together to create a color called for in a particular cake.) They are available in 1½- and 5-pound boxes. You should decide how much of each color to buy; this depends on what cakes you plan or are likely to make. One argument for buying 5-pound boxes is that properly stored, the fondant will last for 1 year.

If you buy another brand of fondant, use the pictures that accompany the cakes to determine the closest approximation to the desired color.

Note that Satin Ice makes two white fondants, vanilla and buttercream. When I call for white fondant in these recipes, I mean the vanilla variety.

- There is a list of ingredients, tools, and equipment included for each recipe. But there are certain items you will need for all recipes, so they are not listed. These are:

  - cornstarch or powdered (10X) sugar for dusting your work surface whenever you are rolling out fondant (see page 199), or as otherwise indicated
  - a turntable
  - a cake icing spatula
  - a polyurethane or ball-bearing rolling pin
  - a smoother
  - a doily-lined cardboard circle

Two Basic Fondant Cakes

As with the progression of steps that leads from cupcakes to full-size cakes, I suggest making a simple fondant cake first, then moving on to more intricate, complex designs. The Dot and Bow and Groovy Girl cakes are ones we use to teach new decorators the ways of fondant at Carlo's, so they're a good place for you to start as well. As you can see, both of these cakes are very makeable, even by first timers.

Dot and Bow Cake

MAKES ONE 9-INCH CAKE

EDIBLES

Two 9-inch cakes, frosted and filled with your choice of filling
4 cups white Decorator's Buttercream (page 154) in a pastry bag fitted
    with the #6 star tip
3 pounds pink fondant
14 ounces dark-chocolate fondant
About 1 cup Chocolate Fudge Frosting (page 313) or brown buttercream
    in a pastry bag fitted with the #6 plain interchangeable tip

TOOLS AND EQUIPMENT

Strip cutter
Water pen or pastry brush
½-inch, 1-inch, and 1½-inch punches
Steamer

1. Prepare the cake: On a turntable, prepare a double-layer cake on a doily-lined cardboard circle, filling it with the filling of your choice and dirty-icing it (see page 197).
2. Cover the cake with fondant: Drape the cake with pink fondant, smooth it in place with the smoother, and trim it (see page 201).
3. Make the bow:

   - Roll the dark-chocolate fondant out to a ⅛-inch-thick rectangle about 6 by 10 inches.
   - Set the cutter to 1½ inches and cut:

     - One 10-inch strip
     - One 2½-inch strip
     - Two 5-inch strips

- Turn the 10-inch strip over and use the water pen to apply a thin layer of water to the center inch.
- Lift the outer ends of the strip and bring them to the center, setting them down end to end and forming loops. Press down gently to make sure they adhere to the damp center portion of the strip.
- Turn over the 2½-inch strip and use the water pen to dampen the entire upward-facing surface. Set it between the loops, perpendicular to the looped 10-inch strip.
- Put your thumb and index fingers in the loops and flip the ribbon over. Fold the 2½-inch center strip over and dab with water to seal it neatly around the center of the bow.
- Flip the two 5-inch strips over and cut 1-inch triangles at one end of each strip to make them look like the ends of ribbons.

4. Affix the bow to the cake:

- Position the 5-inch strips like ribbons a few inches from one edge of the cake, leaving room for the bow, and positioning the triangle-ends farthest from where the bow will rest. Use the water pen to cause the ribbons to ripple, fixing them to the cake in two or three places for support.
- Position the bow toward the top of the cake, alongside the ribbons, fixing it in place with a dab of water.

5. Make polka dots: Use the punches to make polka dots of varying sizes in the remaining rolled-out dark/chocolate fondant, then use the water pen to affix them to the top and sides of the cake.

6. Steam the cake (optional): Steam the cake, paying particular attention to the bow and dots, to make the elements look clean and shiny.

7. Pipe a border around the base: Use the chocolate fudge frosting bag, rotate the turntable, and pulse the bag to pipe a small shell border around the bottom of the cake.

Groovy Girl Cake

EDIBLES

Two 9-inch cakes, filled with your choice of filling
4 cups white Decorator's Buttercream (page 154) in a pastry bag fitted
*   with the #6 star tip*
3 pounds purple fondant
7 ounces pink fondant
7 ounces pastel green fondant
7 ounces yellow fondant
2 ounces dark-chocolate fondant
1 cup yellow buttercream in a pastry bag fitted with the #6
*   interchangeable tip*

TOOLS AND EQUIPMENT

Steamer
Daisy cutters, assorted sizes
Water pen or pastry brush

1. Prepare the cake: On a turntable, prepare a double-layer cake on a doily-lined cardboard circle, filling it with the filling of your choice and dirty-icing it (see page 197).
2. Cover the cake: Drape the cake with purple fondant, smooth it in place with the smoother, and trim it (see page 201).
3. Steam the cake: Use the steamer to steam the fondant and make it shiny.
4. Make daisies:

   • Roll out the pink, pastel green, yellow, and dark-chocolate fondant ⅛ inch thick.

- Use the daisy cutters to cut daisies of various sizes out of each color fondant.
- Overlap the daisies, including different color daisies in each stack and using a water pen to glue them to each other, then onto the cake. Make sure to have one or two overlapping daisies flop from the top to the side of the cake.

5. Pipe a border around the base: Using the yellow buttercream, rotate the turntable and pulse the bag to pipe a shell border around the bottom of the cake.

THEME CAKES

Now that you've had a chance to get comfortable with fondant, try your hand at some of the theme cakes like the ones we make on *Cake Boss*.

Many of the following cakes appeared on the show in larger form. To set you up for success at home, I've scaled them all down—most are presented here as 9-inch cakes or as relatively small rectangles or hearts.

Most of the cakes are meant for a particular season or holiday, so I've arranged them more or less in chronological order as the events occur in the year.

Grown-Up Birthday Cosmo Cake

I developed this as a birthday cake for grown-ups, specifically women in the late 1990s, at the height of the popularity of the show *Sex and the City*. A lot of young women in and around Hoboken related to Carrie and her pals, and more and more of them came in looking for a special event cake for birthdays and bachelorette parties. So I devised this cake featuring the iconic cocktail, the Cosmopolitan.

At Carlo's, we use a mold to make the martini glass; but you can simply make one in the "freestyle" manner described here.

EDIBLES
Two 9-inch cakes, filled with your choice of filling
*4 cups white Decorator's Buttercream (page 154) in a pastry bag fitted
    with the #7 interchangeable plain tip*
3 pounds white or ivory fondant
Pearl luster dust
Pink petal dust
4 ounces green fondant
1 ounce lime-green fondant (see Note)
4 ounces black fondant
4 ounces pink fondant
½ cup red buttercream in a parchment pencil (see page 185)

TOOLS AND EQUIPMENT
Parchment paper
Paintbrush
*½-inch, ¾-inch, 1-inch, 1¼-inch, 1½-inch, 1¾-inch, and 2-inch
    punches*
Water pen or pastry brush
X-Acto knife or sharp, thin-bladed knife, such as a paring knife
Steamer

1. Prepare the cake: On a turntable, prepare a double-layer cake on a doily-lined cardboard circle, filling it with the filling of your choice. Dirty-ice the cake without the tip; see page 197.
2. Cover the cake with fondant: Drape the cake with white fondant, smooth it in place with the smoother, and trim it (see page 201). Do not return the unused fondant to the tub; you will need it to make the cocktail.
3. Make the Cosmopolitan:

   - Start with a 3-ounce piece of white fondant. Break off two thirds of it and roll it into a ball. Flatten it slightly and shape it into a triangle wedge.
   - Take another small piece of the white fondant and roll it into a coil 2 inches long and ¼ inch in diameter; this will be the stem. Use the remaining fondant to make a "home-plate"–shaped piece that will become the base of the glass.
   - Working on a sheet of parchment paper, arrange the pieces into a glass.

4. Color the Cosmopolitan: Use a paintbrush to brush pearl luster dust over the surface of the glass and give it a sugary shine. Brush pink petal dust on the vessel portion of the glass, leaving a ½-inch "lip" at the top.
5. Affix the glass to the cake: Pipe a dab or two of buttercream to the cake where the top of the glass will go, and gently press the vessel onto it, gluing it in place. Repeat with the stem and then the base to form the glass on the top of the cake.

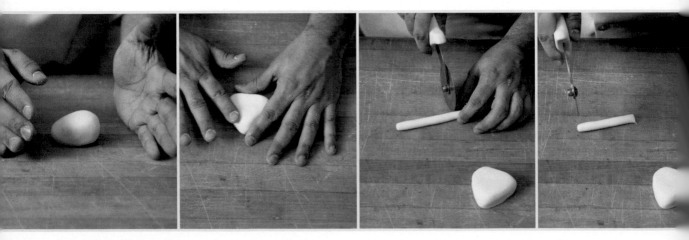

6. Make the lime: Roll out a small piece of green fondant to ⅛ inch thick. Punch out a 1¾-inch ring, then punch out the center with a 1½-inch ring to create the peel. Roll out a small piece of lime-green fondant and punch out a 1½-inch circle. Apply water to the edge of the lime-green circle with a water pen and put the lime-green circle into the green ring.

7. Affix the lime to the glass: Use the X-Acto knife to make an incision that runs halfway up the lime. Pipe a dab of buttercream onto the rim of the glass, and twist the lime onto the rim, gluing it in place with the buttercream.

8. Make polka dots: Roll out the black, green, and pink fondant to ⅛-inch sheets (the shape doesn't matter). Dust them with cornstarch. Punch out polka dots and rings.

- Make polka dots by using punches ranging from ½-inch to 2-inch circles.
- Make rings by punching out circles, then punching out a circle within the circle using a smaller punch; for example, by punching a 1¾-inch circle, then punching out the center with a 1½-inch ring or 1¼-inch ring (the edges of different circles can vary). Save the punched-out center piece for use as a polka dot.

9. Steam the cake: Steam the cake all over, including the glass and lime to set their color and make them shiny. While it is still misty, arrange the circles and polka dots decoratively on the top and sides of the cake, being sure to drape some over the edge, gently pressing them onto the fondant. Steam the cake again to fix the circles and dots onto the cake. Be sure to leave room to write Happy Birthday.

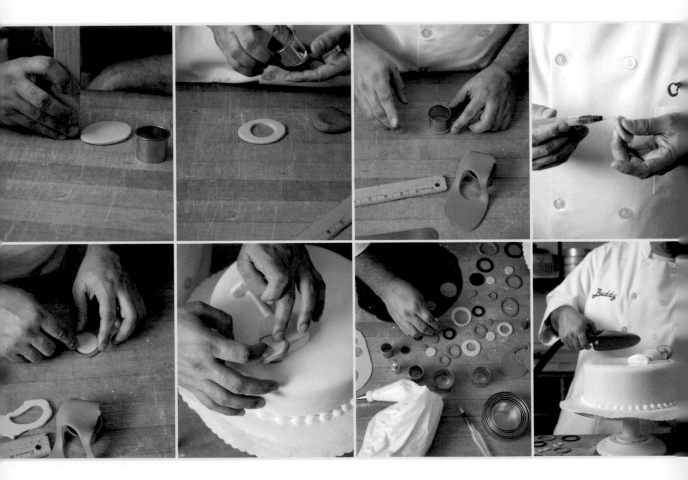

10. Write Happy Birthday: Use the parchment pencil to write Happy Birthday on the cake.
11. Pipe a border around the base: Affix the #7 plain interchangeable tip to the white buttercream bag. Rotate the turntable and pulse the bag to pipe a small shell border around the bottom of the cake.

Note: Make the lime-green fondant by kneading together ½ ounce each of green and yellow fondant.

Happy Birthday, Baby.

A Cake for Guys

For a guy's cake, change the Cosmopolitan to a Martini, using green petal dust instead of pink, replacing the lime with an olive fashioned from dark green fondant, and making the polka dots and rings out of masculine colors such as blue, green, and black. If you like, make a cigar out of dark-chocolate fondant and glue it to the cake just beneath the Martini.

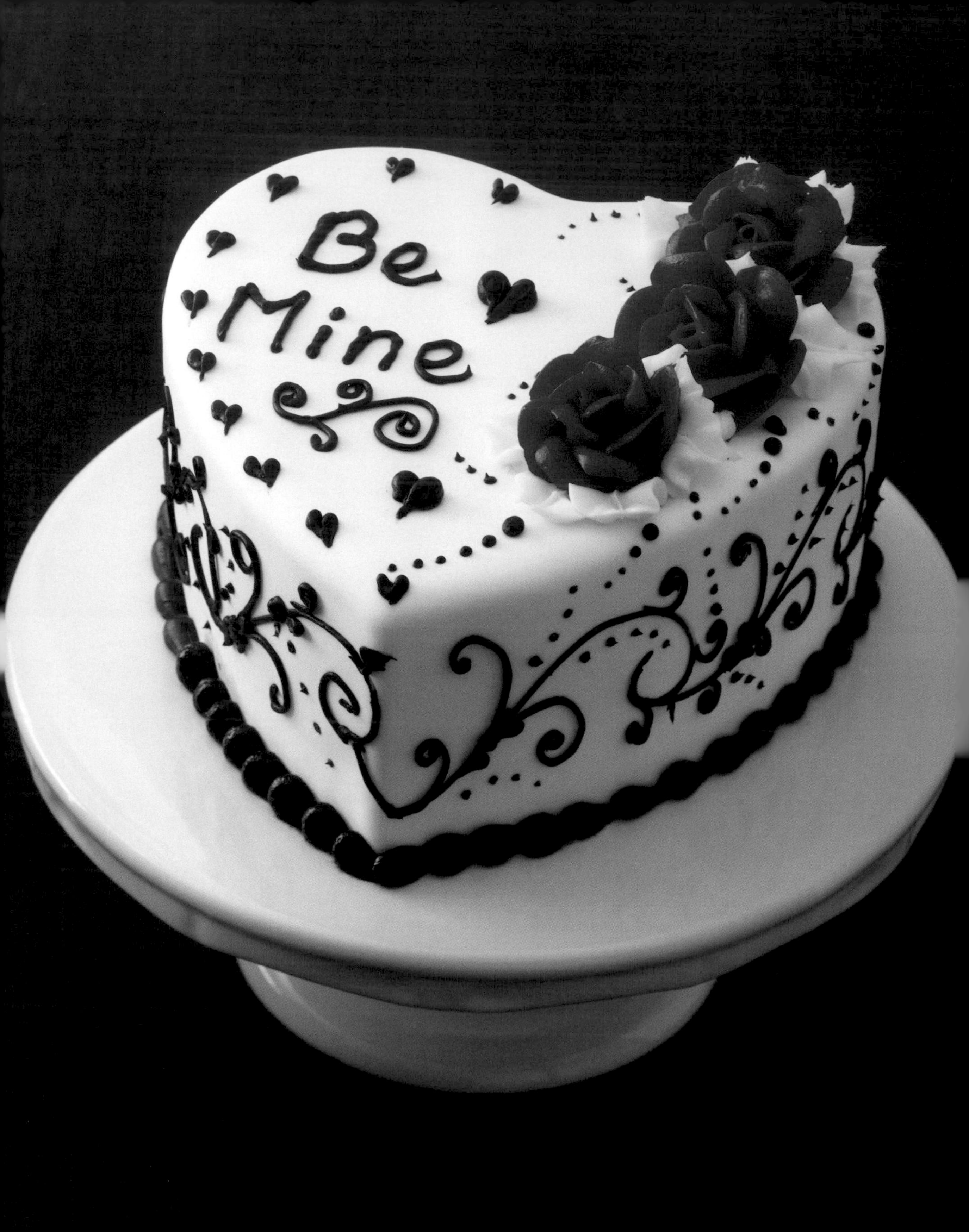
Be Mine

Valentine's Day Cake

Valentine's Day is one of the most sacred days for a cake decorator because of how pressure-filled it is for our customers. I consider it an honor when somebody decides to make our creations a token of affection for his or her loved one and decides to go with a cake instead of (or in addition to) long-stemmed roses and a box of chocolates. As a result, our Valentine's Day cakes are almost like mini wedding cakes, featuring some of the same design touches, namely filigree piping and buttercream roses. If you have any ambition to make wedding cakes, or if you just want to really show your love for somebody, make this cake.

Note that heart cakes can be made with the recipes for vanilla and chocolate cakes on pages 296 and 298; see also page 295.

EDIBLES
One heart-shaped cake, filled with your choice of filling
4½ cups white Decorator's Buttercream (page 154) in a pastry bag fitted with the #67 interchangeable leaf tip
3 pounds white fondant
1½ cups black buttercream in a pastry bag fitted with the #3 plain interchangeable tip
1 cup red buttercream in a pastry bag fit with the #126 rose tip
½ cup black buttercream in a parchment pencil (see page 185)

TOOLS AND EQUIPMENT
Parchment paper

1. Prepare the cake: On a turntable, prepare a double-layer heart cake on a doily-lined cardboard circle, filling it with the filling of your choice. Dirty-ice the cake without the tip (see page 197).
2. Cover the cake with fondant: Drape the cake with white fondant, smooth it in place with the smoother, and trim it (see page 201).

3. Pipe filigree patterns around the cake: Rotating the turntable, use the black buttercream bag to "draw" on the side of the cake in a wave pattern all the way around. Embellish the pattern with "9" and "6" figures, then with series of shrinking dots, a progression from larger to smaller dots.

4. Pipe a shell border around the base: Rotate the turntable and, using the same black buttercream bag and tip, pulse the bag to pipe a black shell border around the bottom of the cake.

5. Make the roses: Use the red buttercream bag to make three buttercream roses (see page 164) and arrange them along the right contour of the heart. Affix the #67 interchangeable leaf tip to the white buttercream bag and pipe

leaves around and between the roses. Decorate with black dots using the same bag and tip you used to decorate the side of the cake.

6. Write "Be Mine": Use the parchment pencil to write Be Mine in black icing along the left contour of the heart. Embellish it by drawing little hearts with the pencil.

Love Conquers All!

Easter Basket

Kids love this Easter-themed cake that captures the colors, energy, and fun of an Easter egg hunt.

EDIBLES
Two 9-inch cakes, filled with your choice of filling
4 cups white Decorator's Buttercream (page 154) in a pastry bag fitted
*   with the #6 star tip*
3 pounds pastel green fondant
3 ounces baby blue fondant
3 ounces lavender fondant
3 ounces baby pink fondant
3 ounces white fondant
3 ounces pastel yellow fondant
2 cups green buttercream in a pastry bag fitted with the #133 grass tip
½ cup pastel color (your choice) buttercream in a parchment pencil (page
*   185), optional*
20 to 25 jelly beans, assorted colors

TOOLS AND EQUIPMENT
Strip cutter, with ruffled-edge attachment if possible
¼-inch punch
Oval cutter (2¼ inches long)

1. Prepare the cake: On a turntable, prepare a double-layer cake on a doily-lined cardboard circle, filling it with the filling of your choice and dirty-icing it (see page 197).
2. Cover the cake with fondant: Drape the cake with pastel green fondant, smooth it in place with the smoother, and trim it (see page 201).

3. Make Easter eggs: Roll rectangles of baby blue, lavender, baby pink, and white fondant, ¼ inch thick and roughly 3 by 7 inches. Roll out small pieces of the same colors of fondant into squares, adding pastel yellow, and cut ¼-inch strips with a strip cutter, making some with ruffled edges if you have the proper attachment, and ¼-inch circles with a punch. Roll over the pieces with a rolling pin. Lay the dots and stripes over the 3 by 7-inch rectangles and roll over them with a pin to make patterned fondant. Use an oval cutter to cut eggs from the squares. You should have 12 to 14 eggs.

4. Decorate the side of the cake: Affix the eggs along the side of the cake at various heights and angles, piping dabs of buttercream to hold them in place.

5. Create the grassy borders: Take the green buttercream bag in hand and squeeze-and-pull "grass" around the border, varying the height to come up to the bottom of each egg.

6. Finish the top of the cake: Use dabs of white buttercream to fix the remaining eggs to the top of the cake, confining yourself to one side. Squeeze-and-pull grass around the eggs on that side of the cake. (If you like, use the parchment pencil to write Happy Easter on the other half.)
7. Decorate the cake with "Easter eggs": Arrange the jelly beans in the grass and around the border to further represent Easter eggs. (If you don't have any jelly beans on hand, you can make them out of fondant.)

Happy Easter!

Mother's Day Cake

MAKES ONE 8-INCH SQUARE CAKE (3 LAYERS)

This cake started its own trend at Carlo's Bake Shop—the "presents" trend.

I wanted to do something different for Mother's Day one year, and it hit me that it would be fun to reverse expectations and come up with a cake that was square instead of round. When I think of Mother's Day, I think of giving your mother a present, so my next thought was to make a cake that looked like a gift.

The result exceeded my wildest dreams, both the execution—this cake really does look like a present—and its popularity. People couldn't get enough of these cakes, and it wasn't long before we began making them for different occasions, each with its own color scheme. Next to Mother's Day, Christmas became a very popular time for this cake.

EDIBLES
Three 8-inch-square, 2-inch high cakes, filled with your choice of filling
6 cups white Decorator's Buttercream (page 154) in a pastry bag fitted
*   with the #8 plain interchangeable tip*
4 pounds pink fondant
3 pounds white fondant

TOOLS AND EQUIPMENT
14-inch square wooden platform, about ¼ inch thick
3-inch peg or a 3-inch-high can
Pastry brush
Kitchen scissors
X-Acto knife, or sharp, thin-bladed knife such as a paring knife
Steamer
Strip cutter
Water pen
Glue gun
58 inches ¼-inch-wide ribbon

1. Prepare the cake: Set the wooden square on your turntable. Top with an 8-inch cardboard square and prepare a triple-layer 8-inch-square cake (three layers of cake, two of frosting, for a 4½-inch-high cake) on the square, filling it with the filling of your choice and dirty-icing it without the tip (see page 197).
2. Cover the cake: Drape the cake with pink fondant, smooth it in place with the smoother, and trim it (see page 201). Do not return the unused fondant to the tub; you will need it to make the "box top."
3. Score the cake: Use a 3-inch peg as a guide to score the side of the cake, rolling it around the perimeter of the cake to mark where the box top will go. (If you do not have a peg, use another 3-inch-high object such as a can of food.) Be sure to use the platform for support to ensure an even scoring.
4. Create the box top: Apply a second layer of fondant to the top of the cake: Roll out a piece of pink fondant to ¼ inch thick and cut out a 12-inch square. Use a pastry brush to brush water above the score line and over the top of the cake. (A brush is better than a water pen here because of the large surface area involved.) Lay the fondant square evenly over the top and bring it down the side of the cake, conforming it to the cake. Trim as much of the excess as you can with scissors, and press the fondant down on the cake. It will hang a bit lower than the score line. Use the peg to again score over the score line, then use the X-Acto knife to follow the score line, turning the turntable to cut away any remaining excess fondant. Be very careful not to cut through the bottom layer of fondant.
5. Steam the cake: Steam the cake all over with the steamer to give the box top and box a nice, shiny, uniform look.

6. Fashion a frame around the cake: Attach the #8 plain tip and pipe some white buttercream onto the wood around the cake. Spread it out with a cake icing spatula. Cut four strips of fondant, each 14 by 4 inches, and lay them on the platform around the cake. (After laying down the first piece, trim each successive piece prior to laying it down to keep from overlapping them; you want them to be flush with each other.) Steam the seams where the pieces meet and gently press together with your fingers to smooth out the seam.

7. Make and apply streamers: Roll out about half the white fondant to at least 18 inches long and 6 inches wide. Use the strip cutter to cut four 18-inch-long strips, each 1½ inches wide, and cross them over the top of the cake. Press down to adhere the streamers to the cake.

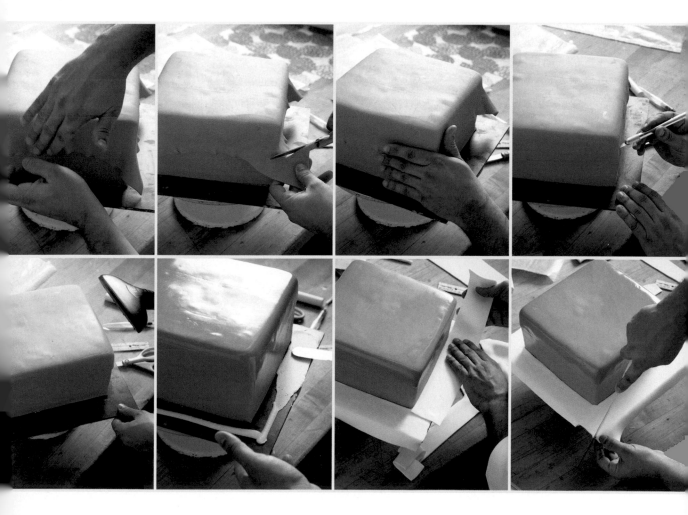

8. Make the bow:

- Roll all remaining white fondant out to a ¼-inch-thick rectangle about 6 inches by 9 inches.
- With the strip cutter still set to 1½ inches, cut:

  - One 9-inch strip
  - One 3-inch strip
  - Two 6-inch strips

- Turn the 9-inch strip over and use the water pen to apply a thin layer of water to the center inch.
- Lift the outer ends of the strip and bring them to the center, setting them down end to end and forming loops. Press down gently to make sure they adhere to the damp center portion of the strip.

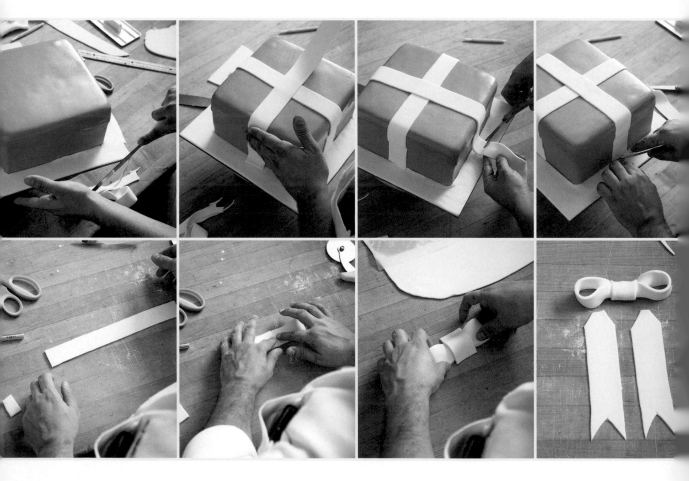

- Turn over the 3-inch strip and use the water pen to dampen the entire upward-facing surface. Set it between the loops, perpendicular to the looped 9-inch strip.
- Put your thumb and index fingers in the loops and flip the ribbon over. Fold the 3-inch center strip over and dab with water to seal it neatly around the center of the bow.
- Flip the two 6-inch strips over and cut 1-inch triangles at one end of each strip to make them look like the ends of ribbons.

9. Affix the bow to the cake:

- Position the 6-inch strips like ribbons extending from the center of the cake, where the streamers cross, and positioning the triangle-ends farthest from where the bow will rest. Use the water pen to cause the ribbons to ripple, fixing them to the cake in two or three places for support.
- Position the bow in the center of the cake, where the ribbons and streamers meet, fixing it in place with a dab of water.

10. Pipe a border around the base: Using the decorator's buttercream, rotate the turntable and squeeze-and-pull a dot border around the bottom of the cake.

11. Apply the ribbon: Use a glue gun to apply ribbon to the edge of the platform. Do not cut until you have applied the ribbon all the way around it.

Happy Mother's Day!

Graduation Cake

Whether it's graduation from high school or college, this cake is the perfect way to honor somebody who's worked hard and crossed the academic finish line.

Note that to make the tassel you will need a clay gun, an extruding tool with interchangeable discs that allow you to create all kinds of shapes by simply applying pressure to the tool.

EDIBLES
Three 9-inch cakes filled with your choice of filling
4 cups white Decorator's Buttercream (page 154) in a pastry bag fitted
    with the #6 star tip
3 pounds black fondant
1 cup black buttercream in a pastry bag fitted with the #6
    interchangeable tip
4 ounces gold fondant (see Note)

TOOLS AND EQUIPMENT
Serrated knife
8-inch cardboard square
Pizza cutter
Clay gun fitted with a 6-hole disc
Water pen

1. Prepare the cake: On a turntable, prepare a triple-layer cake on a doily-lined cardboard circle, filling it with the filling of your choice, *but do not dirty-ice it yet.*
2. Trim the cake: Use a serrated knife to trim the cake into a dome, creating a base on which the cap will sit.

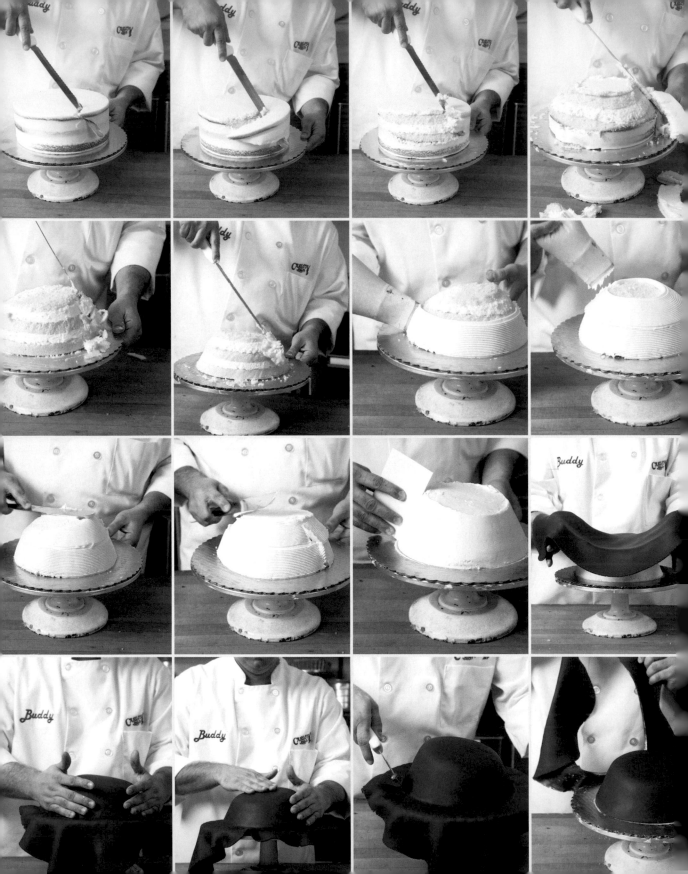

3. Cover the cake with fondant: First, dirty-ice the cake (see page 197). Then drape the cake with black fondant, smooth it in place with the smoother, and trim it (see page 201). Don't return the excess fondant to its storage container; you will need much of it to encase the mortarboard.

4. Prepare the mortarboard: Gather up the excess black fondant, knead it together, and roll it out to ⅛ inch thick. Pipe white buttercream on one side of the cardboard square. Lay the fondant over the board and use a pizza cutter to trim around it. Pipe white buttercream over the other side and along the edges, reroll the fondant, and cover the other side, this time coming down along the sides of the square. Use the pizza cutter to cut off the excess.

5. Affix the mortarboard to the cake: To fix the cap to the cake, pipe some white buttercream onto the top of the cake and lean the mortarboard on it.
6. Pipe a border around the base: Using the black buttercream, rotate the turntable and pulse the bag to pipe a small shell border around the bottom of the cake.

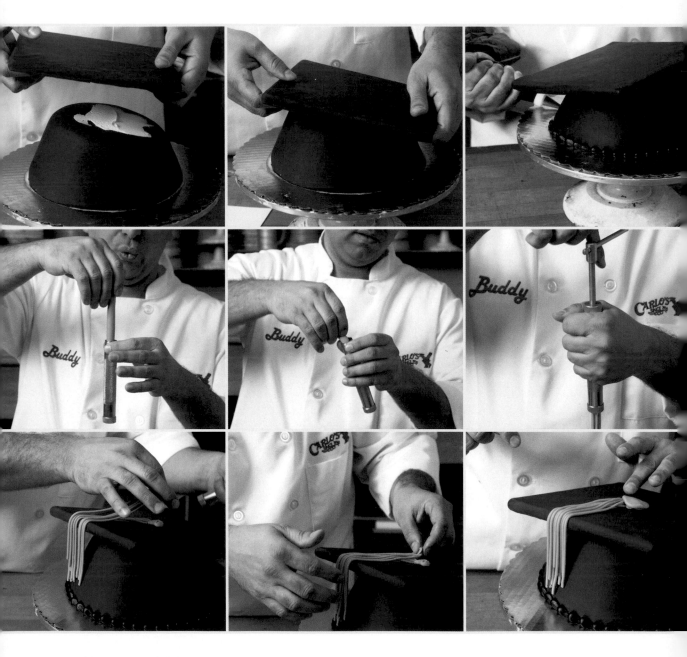

7. Make the tassel: Break off a small piece of the gold fondant and set it aside. Put the remaining gold fondant in the clay gun and turn the handle to create the tassel, processing 2 sets of strands. Use a water pen to glue them to the cap. Roll the small piece of fondant that was set aside into a ball and flatten into a button. Affix the gold button to the cap at one end of the tassels with a dab of water or white icing.

Note: Make the gold fondant by kneading together 3 ounces yellow and 1 ounce dark/chocolate fondant.

Good Luck, Graduate!

Father's Day Cake

I have to be honest: I was a little ticked off when I came up with this cake. Every year, Carlo's Bake Shop is twice as busy for Mother's Day as Father's Day. Now, I love Mother's Day as much as the next guy, but as a dad, and as a guy who loves his dad, this inequality really got under my skin and made me want to create a cool cake for Father's Day.

I decided to play with the quintessential Father's Day gift, a tie.

The guys at the bakery love making this cake—our profession is often thought of as a girly pursuit because so many of the designs we pump out are defined by frilly accents, flowers, and so on. In addition to being fun to make and serve, this masculine cake combats that image.

EDIBLES

13 by 9 by 2-inch cake, cut in half to make two 6½ by 9-inch layers, filled with your choice of filling

4 cups white Decorator's Buttercream (page 154) in a pastry bag fitted with the #6 interchangeable plain tip

3 pounds baby blue fondant

2½ ounces yellow fondant

2½ ounces dark green fondant

3 ounces white fondant

TOOLS AND EQUIPMENT

X-Acto knife or other sharp, thin-bladed knife, such as a paring knife

Strip cutter

Water pen or pastry brush

Steamer

Pizza cutter

Stitching tool

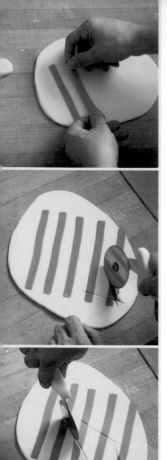

1. Prepare the cake: On a turntable, prepare a double-layer rectangular cake on a doily-lined cardboard rectangle, filling it with the filling of your choice and dirty-icing it without the tip (see page 197).

2. Cover the cake with fondant: Drape the cake with baby blue fondant, smooth it in place with the smoother, and trim it (see page 201).

3. Make the tie:

   • Roll a small piece of yellow fondant out and use the X-Acto knife to cut an oval, 9 inches at its widest point and ¼ inch thick.

   • Roll out a small piece of dark green fondant and cut strips ½ inch wide with a strip cutter. Use a water pen or pastry brush to affix the stripes to the yellow oval, ½ inch apart. Roll over the oval with a rolling pin to embed the stripes into the oval.

   • Use the X-Acto knife to cut a tie out of the striped fondant; the tie should be 5 inches long and 2 inches wide at its widest point.

   • Make the tie's knot by rolling a small piece of yellow fondant into a ball and pressing down on it to flatten it slightly. Use a water pen to fix a strip of dark green fondant to the ball, cutting off any excess.

4. Make the collar: Roll out a piece of white fondant into a narrow strip, ¼ inch thick and 8½ inches long. Set a strip cutter to 1 inch and cut a strip out of the fondant. Set it on top of the cake loosely and bend to shape it into a collar, then carefully remove the collar. Steam the surface of the cake, oversteaming a bit to dampen it. Return the collar to the cake, reestablish the correct position, and press it down onto the surface. (The moist surface will allow you to move the collar on the cake before pressing it down into place.)

5. Affix the tie and knot to the cake: While the surface is still damp, apply the knot and then the tie to the cake, making sure the end of the tie drapes slightly over the edge.

6. Make the pocket: Roll out baby blue fondant into a 2-inch square, ⅛ inch thick. Use a pizza cutter to cut the fondant into a "home plate" shape, simulating a shirt pocket. Cut a 2 by ¼-inch strip out of the fondant and use a water pen or pastry brush to fix it to the pocket. Use a stitching tool to dock small holes all around the border to simulate stitching.

7. Steam the right side of the shirt and carefully affix the pocket to

BUDDY VALASTRO

the shirt, making sure the sides are parallel to the top and side of the cake. Gently press the pocket in place to help it adhere.

8. Steam the cake: Steam the cake again to fix the design elements to the cake and dissipate any lingering cornstarch.

9. Pipe a border around the base: Take the white buttercream bag in hand, fitted with the #6 tip, and pulse to pipe a shell border around the bottom of the cake.

For All the Dads Out There!

Summary Beach Cake

One of the great things about living in the Northeast is that we really get to experience all the seasons, each arriving with its own excitement, which I love trying to capture in a cake. This one brings to life all the fun in the sun that everyone associates with summer by conjuring a beach scene—blue fondant stands in for water, brown sugar is sand, and coral piping along the sides represents the ocean's depths.

If you can find them, I suggest purchasing ready-made edible sandals and surfboards, but by all means you can make those and other summery shapes (starfish, seashells) out of fondant if you like.

EDIBLES

Two 9-inch cakes, filled with your choice of filling
5 cups white Decorator's Buttercream (page 154) in a pastry bag fitted with the #6 interchangeable tip
White, blue, and green fondant, a total of 3 pounds
1½ cups light brown sugar
½ cup blue piping gel, available in prepackaged tubes
½ cup purple buttercream in a pastry bag fitted with the #4 plain interchangeable tip
2 umbrellas, 2 sandals, and 2 surfboards (purchased or fashioned from fondant; see headnote)

1. Prepare the cake: On a turntable, prepare a double-layer cake on a doily-lined cardboard circle, filling it with the filling of your choice and dirty-icing it without the tip (see page 197).
2. Cover the cake with fondant:

   - Gather a total of 3 pounds of aquatic-toned fondant such as white, blue, and green. Twist and knead the colors together until they are marbled and streaked. Gather the fondant into an egg-shaped mound.

- Cut the egg in half lengthwise; the inside should look like a marble. Roll out the fondant and cover the cake (see page 201). Note that you will have about 2 pounds of extra fondant; save it for another beach cake, or knead it together until it forms a uniform shade of blue; seal it in an airtight plastic bag and save it for another use.

3. Apply the sand: Fit the white buttercream bag with the #6 tip and pipe lines of buttercream over the top and side of one third of the cake. Use a cake icing spatula to make a wavy pattern in the icing. Sprinkle brown sugar over the icing evenly to create a "sand" effect; you will not use all the sugar.

4. Create the water: Apply blue piping gel to the top but not the sides of the cake in a shoreline pattern to create a water effect.

5. Pipe a border around the base: Rotate the turntable and pulse the white decorator's buttercream bag to pipe a small shell border around the bottom of the cake.

6. Pipe the coral: Pipe purple buttercream "coral" along the side of the cake.

7. Decorate the cake with seasonal tokens: To complete the beach vibe, stick 2 umbrellas and 2 surfboards in the sand, and rest 2 sandals beside each other in the sand.

Surf's Up!

Fourth of July Cake

MAKES ONE 9-INCH CAKE

As Carlo's Bake Shop has become more and more popular over the years, we developed a great need for cakes that could be easily replicated by anybody who worked in the shop, even our newbies. This cake was developed with that in mind: a spirited but uncomplicated bit of design that adds up to more than the sum of its parts. The colors and shapes do all the work here, but that hasn't stopped this cake from being popular when Independence Day rolls around every year.

EDIBLES
Two 9-inch cakes, filled with your choice of filling
5 cups white Decorator's Buttercream (page 154) in a pastry bag
    fitted with the #7 interchangeable tip
3 pounds white fondant
8 ounces blue fondant
4 ounces red fondant

TOOLS AND EQUIPMENT
9-inch cardboard circle
Pizza cutter
Strip cutter
Kitchen scissors
Steamer
Star cutters, various sizes
Water pen or pastry brush

1. Prepare the cake: On a turntable, prepare a double-layer cake on a doily-lined cardboard circle, fill it with the filling of your choice, and dirty-ice it without the tip (see page 197). (*Note:* After dirty-icing, keep the butter-cream in the bag for affixing design elements to the cake and creating the shell border.)

2. Cover the cake with fondant: Drape the cake with white fondant, smooth it in place with the smoother, and trim it (see page 201). Do not return the unused fondant to the tub; you will need it to make stars.

3. Make a blue fondant top for the cake: Roll out 8 ounces of blue fondant to a 10-inch square. Lay a 9-inch cardboard circle over the dough and cut around it with a pizza cutter to make a circle. Return any unused fondant to its storage container.

4. Apply the top to the cake: Pipe buttercream onto the top of the cake in concentric circles and spread it out smoothly and evenly with a cake icing spatula. The layer should be thin but completely cover the top of the cake;

this will allow you some flexibility when you apply the top. Carefully slide the cardboard circle under the blue fondant circle and use it to transfer the circle to the top of the cake, sliding it off the circle.

5. Make red flag stripes: Roll red fondant out to a rectangle about 5 inches wide, 15 inches long, and ¼ inch thick. Set a strip cutter to 1¼ inches and cut 12 strips from the fondant.

6. Apply the stripes to the side of the cake: Steam the cake. Working quickly with one strip at a time, let it hang down from the top edge of the cake, and cut off the excess at the bottom with scissors. Press the strip onto the moist cake and repeat with the remaining strips, arranging them 1¼ inches apart. Steam the cake again to fix the stripes to the cake and dissipate any lingering cornstarch.

7. Make the stars: Roll out 2 ounces of white fondant. Use a variety of sizes of star cutters to cut stars. (If you do not have a set of star cutters, you can cut freestyle with a sharp, thin-bladed knife such as a paring knife, but star cutters will make the job much easier.) Apply the stars to the top of the cake with a water pen or brush. Steam the cake again to fix the stars onto the cake.

8. Pipe a border around the base: Rotate the turntable and pulse the white decorator's buttercream bag to pipe a shell border along the bottom of the cake.

God Bless America!

Halloween Frankenstein Cake

This cake has evolved over the years, tracking Carlo's evolution from buttercream-focused to fondant-focused. The cake decorating team at Carlo's came up with the idea of making a monster cake for Halloween, creating our original Frankenstein cake. In time, I developed Dracula and werewolf cakes to expand our offerings; how could I resist? These cakes are a lot of fun to make and kids love them. Making smooth faces and hair with the buttercream was a real chore, but when we turned our attention to fondant, these become much easier to produce.

EDIBLES
Two 9-inch cakes, filled with your choice of filling
4 cups white Decorator's Buttercream (page 154) in a pastry bag
   fitted with the #6 star tip
3 pounds lime-green fondant (see Notes)
3 ounces black fondant
3 ounces white fondant
2 cups Chocolate Fudge Frosting (page 313) in a pastry bag fitted with
   the #6 star tip
1 cup Chocolate Fudge Frosting in a parchment paper pencil (page 185)
   or pastry bag fitted with the #3 plain interchangeable tip

TOOLS AND EQUIPMENT
¾-inch, 1½-inch, and 2½-inch punches
Water pen or brush
⅞-inch poker

1. Prepare the cake: On a turntable, prepare a double-layer cake on a doily-lined cardboard circle, filling it with the filling of your choice and dirty-icing it (see page 197).
2. Cover the cake with fondant: Drape the cake with lime-green fondant, trim it, and smooth it in place (see page 201). Do not store the unused fondant until after you have finished decorating the cake; you will need about 6 ounces of it to make some of Frankenstein's features.

3. Make Frankenstein's eyeballs: Roll a small piece of black fondant out to ⅛ inch thick and punch two ¾-inch circles with a cutter.

4. Make Frankenstein's eyes: Roll white fondant out to ⅛ inch thick and punch two 1½-inch circles with a cutter.

5. Assemble the eyes: Dab some water in the center of the white circles and apply the black circles to them, pressing down gently so they adhere.

6. Make Frankenstein's ears: Roll a small piece of lime-green fondant out ¼ inch thick and punch two 2½-inch circles with a cutter.

7. Make the electrodes: Make some gray fondant by kneading together ½ ounce black fondant and ½ ounce white fondant. Roll the gray fondant out 1 inch thick and punch two ⅞-inch knobs out with the back of a poker.

8. Make Frankenstein's nose: Roll a pinball-size piece of lime-green fondant into a quenelle (elongated egg) shape.

9. Make Frankenstein's mouth: Roll a piece of lime-green fondant into a 3-inch-long coil, ½ inch in diameter.

10. Apply Frankenstein's face: Using a water pen or brush, glue the nose to the side of the cake, then glue the mouth under it, bending it upward. Apply the

eyes next to the nose. Fold the ears and glue them to the side of the head. Finish by gluing the electrodes between the mouth and ears on both sides.

11. Create Frankenstein's hair: Use the chocolate fudge frosting bag to pipe lines of "hair" starting at the far side of the cake and pulling all the way toward you, spiking the hair up over his eyes. Use an up-and-down movement to pipe icing from top to bottom along the sides of the cake, creating a wavy effect.

12. Create Frankenstein's stitch marks: Use the parchment pencil to pipe "stitch marks" under both of Frankenstein's eyes and over his mouth. Finish by piping bushy eyebrows over his eyes.

Notes: Make the lime-green fondant by kneading together 1½ pounds each of yellow and green fondant. If you have only one star tip, assemble the bag of fudge frosting after dirty-icing the cake, being sure to clean and dry the tip after removing it from the buttercream bag.

Happy Halloween! Aaarrrgh!

Thanksgiving Turkey

MAKES ONE 8-INCH BUNDT CAKE

Nothing says Thanksgiving like a turkey, and this cake does a great job of bringing the holiday icon to the dessert course. Note that you need to use a #126 rose tip for all of the colors called for here, so you will need several bags and rose tips. If you don't have enough tips, you do not need to use every color called for, although the more colors you use, the better your turkey will look.

EDIBLES
1 Bundt cake in the flavor of your choosing, 8 inches in diameter and 3 inches deep
Chocolate Fudge Frosting (page 313) in a pastry bag fitted with the #6 star tip
A total of 6 cups white, red, black, yellow, brown, and orange Decorator's Buttercream (page 154), each in its own party bag fitted with the #126 rose tip (see headnote)
¼ cup black Decorator's Buttercream in a parchment pencil (page 185)

TOOLS AND EQUIPMENT
Serrated knife

1. Fill the cake: Pipe the cake full of fudge frosting.
2. Shape the turkey: Use a serrated knife to cut the cake at one edge where the central hole meets the cake. Set the larger piece of the cake, frosting side down, on a doily-lined cardboard circle on your turntable. Pipe a dab of white buttercream and seal the small piece in place in front of the larger piece. Pipe white buttercream over any gaps between the two sections to create a smooth working surface.

3. Pipe the plumage: Pipe red buttercream around the high, open end of the turkey in a ruffle pattern. Moving toward the lower, narrower front end of the cake, pipe a ruffled black ring in front the red, overlapping slightly. Continue in this way, piping overlapping ruffled rings of white, yellow, brown, and orange frosting, until you have reached the very front (narrow end) of the cake, starting over with red if necessary. Be sure to finish with white at the very front of the cake. Then cover over the open back of the cake (that is, where the frosting shows) with overlapping layers of frosting, ideally orange, white, red, and black.

4. Feather the frosting: Pull the edge of a cake icing spatula through the frosting at 1-inch intervals, starting at the back center-top of the cake and pulling all the way forward to the narrow, lower front to create a feathered effect in the icing.

5. Pipe the beak and comb: Using the white buttercream, pull up and out from the bottom front of the cake to make a beak. Use the red buttercream to pipe the comb. Use the parchment pencil to pipe the eyes.

Happy Thanksgiving! Gobble! Gobble!

Autumn Cake

MAKES ONE 9-INCH CAKE

Here's another of our signature seasonal cakes, this one a tribute to the coming of fall, which to me means watching the leaves turn to bright, fiery colors. To replicate those hues on a cake, we use different colored fondants and apply petal dust or luster dust—the same powder we use to paint sugar flowers—to produce a lifelike effect.

Note that the leaves need to air-dry for 24 hours.

EDIBLES
Red, yellow, green, and orange fondant, a few ounces of each totaling 4 ounces
12 to 16 ounces orange fondant for making pumpkins
Red, green, orange, and brown petal dust
Two 9-inch cakes, filled with your choice of filling
5 cups white Decorator's Buttercream (page 154) in a pastry bag fitted with the #6 star tip
3 pounds (combined), ivory and dark-chocolate fondant
Chocolate Fudge Frosting (page 313) or brown buttercream in a pastry bag fitted with the #3 plain interchangeable tip

TOOLS AND EQUIPMENT
Double-sided leaf cutter-veiners, various sizes
Ball tool
Petal pad
Aluminum foil
Dresden tool or sharp, thin-bladed knife such as a paring knife
Water pen or pastry brush

1. Make the leaves:

   - Roll small balls of red, yellow, green, and orange fondant as thin as you possibly can. Use a plunger cutter-veiner, or a cutter and press, to make leaves of varying sizes and colors.
   - Use a ball tool and petal pad to roll the edges of the leaves, causing them to curl. Set the leaves in a single layer on a piece of aluminum foil and let dry at room temperature for 24 hours.
   - When ready to proceed, paint the leaves with petal dust, using red, green, orange, and brown petal dust. Use darker-color dust on the edges of the leaves to accentuate their shape.

2. Prepare the cake: Prepare a double-layer 9-inch cake, filling it with the filling of your choice and dirty-icing it (see page 197).

3. Cover the cake with fondant:

   - Gather a total of 3 pounds of ivory and dark-chocolate fondant. (If you can't find ivory fondant, mix some molasses into white fondant, adjusting the color to your liking; the more molasses, the darker it will be.)
   - Twist and knead them together until they are marbled and streaked. Gather the fondant into an egg-shaped mound.
   - Cut the egg in half lengthwise; the inside should look like a marble. Roll out the fondant and cover the cake (see page 201). Note that you will have about 2 pounds of extra fondant; save it for another autumn cake, or knead it together until it forms a uniform shade of light brown; seal it in an airtight plastic bag and save it for another use.

4. Make the pumpkins: Make 6 to 8 pumpkins by rolling orange fondant into balls, making some the size of Ping-Pong balls and others slightly smaller. Press down on the tops to flatten them slightly and make them plump. Score the pumpkins from top to bottom with a Dresden tool or the back of a paring knife. Fashion small stems from green fondant, curl them, and apply them to the center top of the pumpkins with a dab of water from a water pen or brush.

5. Pipe a border around the base: Rotate the turntable and pulse the chocolate fudge frosting bag to pipe a small shell border around the bottom of the cake.

6. Pipe tree and branch pattern: Use the same bag and tip to pipe a vein-like tree and branch pattern on top of the cake.

7. Affix the leaves to the cake: Stick the leaves to the chocolate fudge piping, adding more as glue if necessary. Set a big leaf in the center of the cake.
8. Decorate with pumpkins: Arrange a few pumpkins around the base of the cake and a few on top.

Chill Out . . . It's Fall!

Baby Shower Cake

I came up with this cake so that moms-to-be could have a special cake for their baby showers and other maternity celebrations.

EDIBLES

Two 9-inch cakes, filled with your choice of filling
4 cups white Decorator's Buttercream (page 154) in a pastry bag
fitted with the #6 plain interchangeable tip
3 pounds yellow fondant
13 ounces white fondant
2½ ounces pastel green fondant
2½ ounces lavender fondant

TOOLS AND EQUIPMENT

Pizza cutter or sharp, thin-bladed knife such as a paring knife
Water pen or pastry brush
Daisy plunger cutter
Circle plunger cutter (¼-inch)
Strip cutter with wavy or frill edge attachment

1. Prepare the cake: On a turntable, prepare a double-layer cake on a doily-lined cardboard circle, filling it with the filling of your choice and dirty-icing it without the tip (see page 197). (*Note:* After dirty-icing, keep white buttercream in the bag for affixing design elements to cake and creating the shell border.)

2. Cover the cake with fondant: Drape the cake with yellow fondant, smooth it in place with the smoother, and trim it (see page 201). (Do not return the fondant to its tub; you will need a small amount, about ½ ounce, for the "ribbon" on the dress.)

3. Make the mom:

- Roll 2 marble-size orbs and one egg-size orb out of white fondant.
- Roll out white fondant, ⅛ inch thick and 8 by 4 inches. Use a pizza cutter or a sharp, thin-bladed knife to cut out a triangle. Drape the triangle over the "breasts" and "belly" and use your hands to help it conform to the shape.
- Carefully pick up the mom and set on one side of the cake. Create a ruffle effect by gluing the folds in place with a dab of water from the water pen or pastry brush.
- Add ribbons to the dress: Cut a ½ by 3-inch strip of pastel green fondant with a ruffled-edge pizza cutter or ruffled-edge strip cutter. Use a water pen or pastry brush to fix it along the waistline on the mom and trim any excess. Repeat, making a ¼ by 6-inch piece, and affix this to the bottom edge of the dress.

4. Make the daisies: Roll a small piece of lavender fondant out to an 8-inch square, ¼ inch thick. Use a daisy plunger cutter to cut out 20 to 24 daisies. Repeat with a small piece of pastel green fondant. Roll out a small piece of yellow fondant to ¼ inch thick and use a circle plunger cutter to punch out small circles. Use a water pen or pastry brush to apply a dab of water to the center of each daisy and press the yellow circles into place, then use the pen to affix the daisies to the cake.

5. Pipe a border around the base: Rotate the turntable and pulse the bag to pipe a small shell border around the bottom of the cake with decorator's buttercream.

6. Add kisses: Use the same icing, bag, and tip to squeeze-and-pull kiss shapes along top edge and side of the cake.

Congratulations, Mom!

Snowflake Winter Wonderland Cake

Another of our seasonal cakes, this one pays tribute to the wonders of winter with snowflakes, frost, and a blue-and-white color scheme. Whether or not you live in the Northeast, I think everybody responds to these images when the holidays roll around. As soon as Thanksgiving comes and goes, I look forward to making this cake, and I hope it might become a similar tradition for you and your family.

EDIBLES
Two 9-inch cakes, filled with your choice of filling
4 cups white Decorator's Buttercream (page 154) in a pastry bag fitted
*   with the #7 interchangeable tip*
3 pounds baby blue fondant
6 ounces white fondant
½ cup crystal or coarse sugar
Pearl luster dust

TOOLS AND EQUIPMENT
Snowflake cutters or plunger cutters, assorted sizes
Paintbrush
Steamer

1. Prepare the cake: On a turntable, prepare a double-layer cake on a doily-lined cardboard circle, filling it with the filling of your choice and dirty-icing it without the tip (see page 197). (*Note:* After dirty-icing, keep the buttercream in the bag for affixing design elements to cake and creating the shell border.)

2. Cover the cake: Drape the cake with baby blue fondant, smooth it in place with the smoother, and trim it (see page 201).

3. Make snowflakes: Roll the white fondant out to a 10-inch square, ⅛ inch

thick. Use large and small snowflake cutters or plungers to make 18 to 20 snowflakes. Use a small brush to paint the flakes with luster dust.

4. Apply frost to the cake: Steam the cake and sprinkle ¼ cup of the sugar to make a 1-inch border around the top edge of the cake; steam it in place. Sprinkle the remaining ¼ cup sugar around the bottom of the cake to make a 2-inch border, then steam it into place.

5. Apply the snowflakes to the cake: Pipe buttercream dabs onto the top and sides of the cake and use it to affix the snowflakes to the cake.

6. Pipe kisses: Use the same bag to squeeze-and-pull kisses around the cake.

Enjoy the Most Wonderful Time of the Year!

Chanukah Cake

MAKES ONE 9-INCH CAKE

I might not have grown up celebrating Chanukah, but I enjoy making this cake, with a huge menorah on top. My favorite effect is the flames, created by putting yellow and orange buttercream in the same pastry bag without having blended them together.

EDIBLES
Two 9-inch cakes, filled with your choice of frosting
5 cups white Decorator's Buttercream (page 154), in a pastry bag fitted with the #6 interchangeable tip
3 pounds light blue fondant (see Note)
½ cup orange buttercream and ½ cup yellow buttercream in a pastry bag fitted with the #27 interchangeable tip
1½ ounces yellow fondant

TOOLS AND EQUIPMENT
Small rectangle of cardboard or poster board
Triangle cutter (1½-inch sides)
Water pen or pastry brush

1. Prepare the cake: On a turntable, prepare a double-layer cake on a doily-lined cardboard circle, filling it with the filling of your choice and dirty-icing it without the tip (see page 197). (*Note:* After dirty-icing, keep white buttercream in the bag for affixing design elements to cake and creating the shell border.)
2. Cover the cake with fondant: Drape the cake with light blue fondant, smooth it in place with the smoother, and trim it (see page 201).
3. Mark the cake for the menorah: Using the white buttercream and #6 interchangeable tip, pipe 9 small dots across the cake, evenly spacing them.

4. Pipe the menorah base: Pipe a small white buttercream triangle at the bottom of the cake, aligning its top tip with the middle dot. Use a small square of cardboard or poster board to smooth out the top of the triangle. Pipe lines of buttercream from the top of the triangle to the other dots, creating the "arms" of the menorah.

5. Pipe the candles: Using white buttercream, pipe small receptacles at the top of each arm of the menorah, then pipe candles from the receptacles to a few inches from the edge of the cake.

6. Pipe a border around the base: Still working with the white buttercream, rotate the turntable and pulse the bag to pipe a small dot border around the bottom of the cake, leaving space between dots.

7. Pipe the flames: Use the yellow and orange buttercream bag to pipe flames at the top of each candle, then pipe small flames between the dots of the border.

8. Make a Star of David: Roll out the yellow fondant and punch out 2 triangles with 1½-inch sides. Use a water pen to moisten the bottom of one triangle and affix it to the other to make a Jewish star, then gently but firmly affix the star to where the arms of the menorah meet the base.

Note: Knead together 1½ pounds each of blue and white fondant to match the color in the photos; you can also use premade blue fondant.

Happy Chanukah!

Santa Christmas Cake

MAKES 1 HEART-SHAPED CAKE

Kids love this Santa cake, made with the ingeniously simple trick of inverting a heart-shaped cake to replicate the shape of Santa's head.

You can personalize your Santa by varying the tips you use to make his eyebrows and beard; for example, using a grass tip produces a hairier beard. Santa's beard, mustache, and eyebrows offer plenty of opportunity to practice your piping by challenging you to go up and down the side of the cake and to create design elements that seem to flow. My advice is not to overstrive when you do this; establish a mental picture of what you want these parts to look like and trust your hands to do the work.

If you like, you can ice this cake with Italian Buttercream (page 314) rather than covering it with white fondant.

EDIBLES
Two-layered heart-shaped cake, filled with your choice of filling
3 pounds white fondant
3 ounces red fondant
6 cups white Decorator's Buttercream (page 154) in a pastry bag fitted with the #32 interchangeable star tip
Blue piping gel
Red piping gel or ½ cup red buttercream in a parchment pencil (see page 185)

TOOLS AND EQUIPMENT
Pizza cutter
#6 interchangeable pastry tip

1. Prepare the cake: On a turntable, prepare a double-layer heart-shaped cake on a doily-lined cardboard circle, filling it with the filling of your choice and dirty-icing it without the tip (see page 197). (*Note:* After dirty-icing, keep

white buttercream in the bag for affixing design elements to cake and creating the border.)

2. Cover the cake with fondant: Drape the cake with white fondant, smooth it in place with the smoother, and trim it (see page 201).

3. Make Santa's hat: Roll out and cut a 10-inch square of red fondant, ⅛ inch thick. Pipe and thinly spread out a layer of buttercream around the point of the heart cake. Lay the red fondant square diagonally so that it points right between the two rounded edges of the heart and rests about 1 inch from the point. Use a pizza cutter to trim away the excess fondant and create the hat. Save the excess fondant.

4. Frame the hat: Rotate the turntable and pulse the buttercream bag with the #32 star tip to pipe a shell border along the bottom edge of the cake. Pipe

sideways up from the base over the top of the cake and down the other side to frame the hat. Then apply a small, swirly dab at the point of the hat.

5. Pipe Santa's mustache and beard: Using the same bag and tip, and beginning at the center of the heart, pipe a moustache, then a beard.

6. Pipe Santa's nose, eyebrows, and beard: Change to the #6 plain interchangeable tip and pipe Santa's nose. Switch back to the star tip and pipe fluffy eyebrows, then the beard.

7. Make Santa's eyes and mouth. Pipe Santa's eyeballs with blue piping gel, then "draw" Santa's mouth in his beard with red piping gel.

Merry Christmas! Ho! Ho! Ho!

Christmas Lights Cake

What's the first thing you think of when you picture Christmas? For me, the quintessential images of the holiday are flashing Christmas tree lights, and red and green everywhere. This cake captures all of that in a festive, colorful design that instantly evokes all the joys of the season.

EDIBLES

Two 9-inch cakes, filled with your choice of filling
4 cups white Decorator's Buttercream (page 154) in a pastry bag
*   fitted with the #6 star tip*
3 pounds white fondant
3 ounces red fondant
3 ounces blue fondant
3 ounces purple fondant
3 ounces yellow fondant
3 ounces green fondant
Silver luster dust
1 cup red buttercream in a pastry bag fitted with the #6 plain
*   interchangeable tip*
1 cup green buttercream in a pastry bag fitted with the #6 plain
*   interchangeable tip*
½ cup red buttercream in a parchment pencil (see page 185)

TOOLS AND EQUIPMENT

Lightbulb cookie cutter
Paintbrush

1. Prepare the cake: On a turntable, prepare a double-layer cake on a doily-lined cardboard circle, filling it with the filling of your choice and dirty-icing it (see page 197).

2. Cover the cake: Drape the cake with white fondant, smooth it in place with the smoother, and trim it (see page 201).
3. Make the lightbulbs: Roll out red, blue, purple, yellow, and green fondant to a thickness of ⅛ inch. Use a lightbulb cutter to punch out three lights from each color. Use a paintbrush to paint silver luster dust on to the lights.
4. Pipe a border around the base of the cake: Rotate the turntable and pulse the red buttercream bag to pipe a small shell border around the bottom of the cake.
5. Pipe light strands around the top of the cake: Rotate the turntable and use steady pressure on the green buttercream bag to pipe a free-form border, weaving on and off the edge of the cake to form strands.
6. Apply the lights: Stick the fondant lightbulbs to the strands.
7. Write "Merry Christmas": Use the parchment pencil to write Merry Christmas.

Merry Christmas to All,
and to All a Good Night!

Animal Safari Cake

MAKES ONE 2-TIER CAKE

This is the most ambitious cake in the book—a two-tiered beauty featuring animal figurines, piped trees and leaves, nature touches such as bushes and rocks, and a waterfall that flows from top to bottom. It looks complicated, but if you take it one step at a time, you might be surprised at how makeable it is, even at home.

This cake also offers a chance to use modeling chocolate (see "Modeling Chocolate," page 283), which can be used to make figurines of just about anything you can think of.

I have broken out the quantities of modeling chocolate, fondant, and icing called for to make each animal—as well as any special tools called for—to make it easy for you to produce the same animals for other cakes, or make more of one than another on this cake.

EDIBLES AND EQUIPMENT FOR THE ANIMALS

FOR THE ELEPHANT OR HIPPO
*3 ounces gray modeling chocolate (make by adding a few drops of black
food coloring to white modeling chocolate and kneading to form gray)*
Toothpick
2 ounces white fondant
2 ounces black fondant
1 ounce pink fondant
Small punches

FOR THE LION
3 ounces orange modeling chocolate
1 ounce white fondant
1 ounce black fondant
*½ cup Chocolate Fudge Frosting (page 313) in a bag fitted with the #133
interchangeable grass tip*

Modeling Chocolate

Modeling chocolate has been a part of some of the most popular cakes on *Cake Boss* because most of the figurines we make are fashioned from it. The truth is that there's no great secret to working with modeling chocolate; it's just like working with clay or Play-Doh—just have fun and do your best to sculpt whatever you want to make for your cake. The more you sculpt, the better you'll get, and if you mess up, you can just knead the chocolate together and start over.

That said, here are some useful tips:

- Modeling chocolate is sold in chocolate (brown) and white. You can color the white with food coloring to create any colors you want, just as with decorator's buttercream.
- Before working with modeling chocolate, microwave it for 10 seconds and briefly knead it to loosen it up.
- When working with modeling chocolate, you need to pay close attention to the temperature of your hands. If they get too warm, they will start to melt the chocolate. If your hands get too warm, dip them in cornstarch to minimize this effect. At the same time, your warm hands can be a useful tool. Just before fusing pieces together with a water pen, rub the modeling chocolate to warm and loosen it.

FOR THE MONKEY
3 ounces brown modeling chocolate
1 ounce ivory fondant
1 ounce white fondant
#10 pastry tip
1¼- and 1-inch circle cutters
Toothpick
Black edible marker

FOR THE GIRAFFE
3 ounces yellow modeling chocolate
Water pen
1 ounce white fondant

2 ounces dark-chocolate fondant
¼- and ½-inch plunger cutters
Black edible marker

FOR THE ZEBRA
1½ ounces ivory modeling chocolate
1½ ounces white fondant
1 ounce pink fondant
Toothpick
1 ounce black fondant
Black edible marker

EDIBLES AND EQUIPMENT FOR THE CAKE

EDIBLES
12 ounces (total) white and black fondant
24 ounces green modeling chocolate
Two 6-inch cakes cut out of sheet cake filled with your choice
    of filling
8 cups white Decorator's Buttercream (page 154) in a pastry bag
    fitted with the #6 star tip
5 pounds ivory fondant
Two 9-inch cakes filled with your choice of filling
3 cups brown buttercream in a pastry bag fitted with the #7
    interchangeable tip
3 cups green buttercream in a pastry bag fitted with the #7
    interchangeable tip
2 cups blue piping gel

TOOLS AND EQUIPMENT
Toothpick
16-inch round wooden board, ¼ inch thick
X-Acto knife or sharp, thin-bladed knife such as a paring knife
Four 5-inch plastic air-conditioning tubes (¾-inch diameter)
    or 4 chopsticks
#133 interchangeable grass tip

1. To make the elephant:

   - Form 4 marble-size pieces of gray modeling chocolate and roll gently into sausage shapes to make the legs. Set them on their ends right next to each other to make the base.
   - Make a small ball of modeling chocolate and roll at the center to produce a head with a trunk, curving it. If desired, affix a small piece of pink fondant to the end with the water pen.
   - Roll a slightly oval-shaped body, larger than the head.
   - Form 3 pea-size pieces of modeling chocolate: roll one into the elephant's tail; flatten the other two to make ears.
   - Roll out the white and black fondants and punch out small circles to make the elephant's eyes and eyeballs (the eyes should be just smaller than the eyeballs), gluing them together with a water pen. Roll 2 tusks out of white fondant.
   - Use a water pen to moisten the top of the elephant's legs and press the

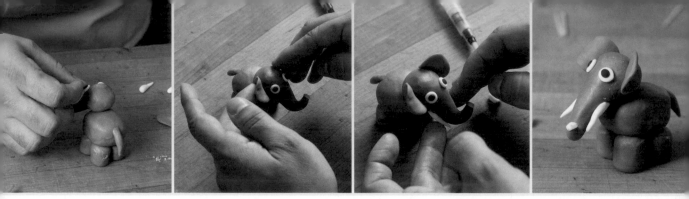

body down on top. Glue the tail on the back. Snap the toothpick in half, stick it in the body toward the front of the head, and use it for support, sticking the head on top. Glue the tusks and eyes to the face and the ears to either side of the head.

2. To make the hippo, follow the same steps, but vary them to make a slightly larger head and body, affixing the ears to the back of the head and fashioning white toenails and pink nostrils and affixing them with a water pen.

3. To make the lion:

   - Fashion a golf ball–size ball of orange modeling chocolate for the body and a smaller ball for the head. Use a water pen to moisten the head and affix it to the body, smoothing it into place.
   - Roll 4 marble-size orange pieces to form the arms and legs and use a water pen to moisten them and affix them to the body.
   - Roll a small orange tail and use a water pen to moisten it and glue it to the back of the body.
   - Use the white and black fondant to make eyes and eyeballs. Make the eyes

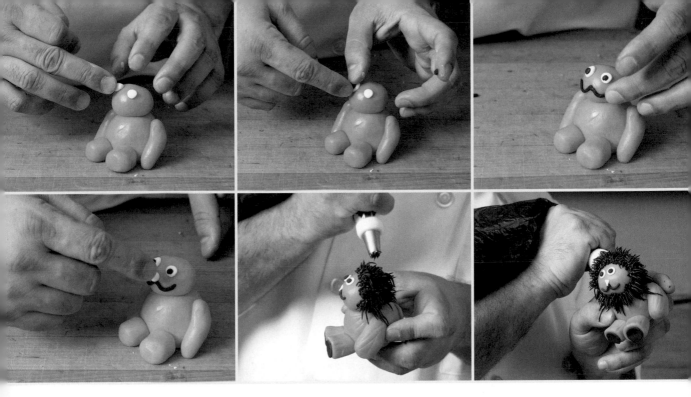

more like little balls, whereas they are flat for the elephant. Use a water pen to glue the eyes and eyeballs together and to glue them to the head. Roll a small white dot for the nose and use a water pen to glue it to the head.

- Roll a very thin coil of black to make a moustache, and glue it on the lion's head, under the nose, with a water pen.
- Pipe the mane with fudge frosting.

4. To make the monkey:

- Roll a Ping-Pong ball–size piece of brown modeling chocolate for the body and a smaller ball for the head. Roll 4 small coils, 2 long and 2 short, for the monkey's arms and legs. Roll out 2 small circles for its ears.
- Mix the ivory fondant with just a pinch of modeling chocolate to make a tan mixture. Roll it out to ⅛ inch thick. Punch out a 1¼-inch circle for the monkey's belly and a 1-inch circle for its face.
- Make 2 eyeballs by punching the white fondant with the tip of a #10 pastry tip.
- Glue the monkey's legs to the lower sides of its body. Glue the 1¼-inch circle (belly) to its stomach and the 1-inch circle (face) to its head. Glue the arms to its sides, bending them to make them wavy. Glue on the ears. Glue on the eyeballs.

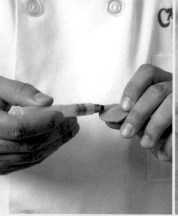

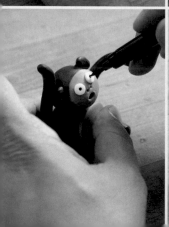

- Use the toothpick to poke small indentations for the monkey's nose and mouth.
- Draw on eye and eyelashes with the edible marker.

5. To make the giraffe:

- Roll 4 marble-size pieces of yellow modeling chocolate and shape them into the legs.
- Roll a long, bulbous body and bend carefully at the top to form the head. Use the water pen to glue the legs to the body.
- Roll small balls that will become the eyes out of white fondant and use a water pen to glue them to the head.
- Roll out the dark-chocolate fondant to ⅛ inch thick and use the ¼-inch and ½-inch plunger cutters to make a total of 18 polka dots. Use the water pen to glue the spots all over the giraffe's body. Also fashion a small, heart-shaped tuft of hair to go on top of the giraffe's head.
- Use the edible marker to draw eyeballs and eyebrows.

6. To make the zebra:

- Knead together the white modeling chocolate and white fondant just until uniformly mixed. Roll 4 marble-size pieces and gently roll them into the legs. Fashion the body and head, then attach the head to the body, smoothing the chocolate where they meet. Make 2 small triangular ears. Make 4 tiny balls that will become the eyes and nostrils of the zebra.
- From the pink fondant, fashion 2 small triangles and use a water pen to glue them inside the ears, then fashion a thin coil and use a water pen to glue it as the zebra's mouth. Use the water pen to glue on the eyes and nostrils, using a toothpick to help set them in place if necessary.
- Fashion a black tail from black fondant and use a water pen to glue it to the back of the zebra.
- Draw eyes on the zebra with the edible marker, then use the marker to draw stripes on its body.

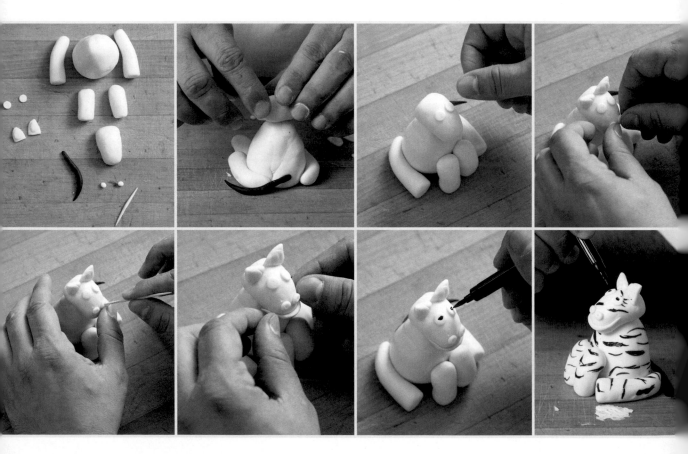

7. To make the rocks: Knead together the white and black fondant and make rocks of varying sizes. The exact ratio of one color to another does not matter, but it's essential that you use more white than black to get gray.

8. To make the bushes: Shape the green modeling chocolate into bushes of varying sizes. Scratch the bushes with a toothpick to texture them. At the bakery, we use a handcrafted wire tool (see picture); if you like, you can fashion one yourself by adapting a paintbrush.

9. Prepare the small cake: On a turntable, prepare a two-layer 6-inch cake, filling it with the filling of your choice and dirty-icing it with white buttercream (see page 197). Cover the cake with ivory fondant, smoothing it with a smoother and trimming it (see page 201). Remove the cake from the turntable and set it aside.

10. Prepare the platform and large cake: Prepare a double-layer 9-inch cake on the wooden board, filling it with the filling of your choice and dirty-icing it with white buttercream.

11. Cover the large cake with fondant: Drape the cake with ivory fondant, letting it flow down and onto the platform. Smooth it in place with the smoother (see page 202), but do not cut off the excess around the cake; instead, let it extend to the edge of the board and cut it flush with the edge. Run the X-Acto knife around the base of the cake where the fondant meets the base, but leave the fondant on the platform in place.

12. Position the upper tier: Center a 6-inch cardboard circle toward the back of the 9-inch cake. Use the X-Acto knife to cut around the circle, creating a shallow indentation to mark where the upper tier will go. Push four tubes

into the circle to support the top cake. (We use a variety of sizes of air-conditioning tubes at Carlo's to support cake tiers; if you cannot get tubes, use chopsticks, cutting them after embedding them into the cake so they are flush with the cake.) Pipe a small amount of white buttercream over the area defined by the pegs and smooth it with a spatula. Set the small cake on top of the larger cake.

13. Pipe the trees: Use the brown buttercream bag to pipe tree branches along the side of both tiers of the cake. Piping trees on the back of the cakes is optional. If you do not have two #7 tips, you will need to move the tip from the brown bag to the green after piping the tree branches; be sure to clean and dry it after removing it from the brown bag.

14. Pipe the leaves: Use the green buttercream bag fitted with the #7 interchangeable tip to pipe shell-shaped leaves on the trees.
15. Create the waterfall: Ice a portion of the top cake with white buttercream, piping down the side, along the bottom of the cake, and down to the base. Smooth the buttercream with a cake icing spatula. Top with blue piping gel and smooth it over with the spatula.
16. Pipe grass all over the cake: Switch to the #133 interchangeable grass tip on the green buttercream bag and squeeze-and-pull a grass border around both tiers of the cake, as well as alongside the waterfall. Vary the angle to create a "wild," natural look.
17. Decorate the cake with bushes and animals: Arrange bushes and animals around the cake, piping a dab of buttercream down before applying each one to hold it in place.
18. Decorate the cake with rocks: Arrange rocks around the cake, being sure to put some in the grass on the side of the cake.

Born to Be Wild!

Basic Cake Recipes

The following recipes produce the basic cakes called for in the book. Because it's the most common size called for throughout the book, the recipe yields indicate two 9-inch cakes, but these recipes can also be used to produce two heart-shaped cakes, a 13 by 9-inch rectangular cake, or two Bundt cakes using 8-inch-wide, 3-inch-deep molds.

Note that oven temperatures differ, so be sure to follow the signs for doneness (not just cooking time); depending on elevation, weather conditions, and other factors, baking times can vary. And remember, unless otherwise indicated, it's a good idea to have all ingredients at room temperature; see the note on mixing on page 33.

Baking Cupcakes

Many of these recipes feature a yield for cupcakes as well. Bake cupcakes at 360°F to prevent them from crowning.

Vanilla Cake

This is a home version of the basic vanilla cake we use at Carlo's. The custard is optional, but really makes the cake unfailingly moist.

2½ cups cake flour, plus more for flouring the cake pans
2 cups sugar, plus more for unmolding the cakes
2 cups Italian Custard Cream (page 315), optional
¾ cup vegetable oil
2¼ teaspoons baking powder
1 teaspoon pure vanilla extract
½ teaspoon fine sea salt
4 extra-large eggs
1 cup whole milk
Unsalted butter (about 2 tablespoons), nonstick spray, or vegetable oil
    may be used for greasing the cake pans

1. Position a rack in the center of the oven, and preheat to 350°F.
2. Put the flour, sugar, custard cream (if using), vegetable oil, baking powder, vanilla, and salt in the bowl of a stand mixer fitted with the paddle attachment. (If you don't have a stand mixer, you can use a hand mixer, but take extra care not to overmix.) Mix on low speed just until the ingredients are blended together, a few seconds, then raise the speed to low-medium and continue to mix until smooth, approximately 1 additional minute.
3. With the motor running, add one egg at a time, adding the next one after the previous one has been absorbed into the mixture. Stop the motor periodically and scrape the bowl from the bottom with a rubber spatula to integrate the ingredients, and return the mixer to low-medium speed.
4. After all the eggs are added, continue to mix for 1 additional minute to ensure the eggs have been thoroughly mixed in. This will help guarantee

that the sugar is dissolved and that the flour has been thoroughly mixed in, which will help produce a luxurious mouthfeel in the final cake.

5. With the motor running on low speed, add the milk, ½ cup at a time, stopping the motor to scrape the sides and bottom between the two additions. Continue to mix for another 1 minute or until the mixture appears smooth. Before baking, be sure the batter is between 70° and 73°F, or the cake will crown. (Test by plunging a kitchen thermometer into the center of the batter; if it is too warm, put the bowl in the refrigerator for a few minutes; if too cool, let it rest at room temperature.)

6. Grease two 9-inch cake pans (2 inches deep) and flour them. (For more, see "To Flour a Cake Pan," below.)

7. Divide the batter evenly between the two cake pans, using a rubber spatula to scrape down the bowl and get as much batter as possible out.

8. Bake until the cake begins to pull from the sides of the pan and is springy to the touch, 25 to 30 minutes.

9. Remove the cakes from the oven and let cool for at least 30 minutes, preferably 1 hour. The cakes should be at room temperature before you remove them from the pan.

10. Put a piece of parchment paper on a cookie sheet, sprinkle with sugar, and one at a time, turn the pans over and turn the cakes out onto parchment; the sugar will keep them from sticking.

Refrigerate or freeze (see page 170) until ready to decorate.

To Flour a Cake Pan

To flour a cake pan, first grease with a thin, even layer of unsalted butter, nonstick spray, or vegetable oil, to coat it just lightly. Add a small fistful of flour (about ¼ cup) to the center of the pan, tip the pan on its side, and rotate the pan to coat the inside with flour. Tap the pan gently on your work surface to loosen the excess flour, and return the excess to your flour container. Tap again and discard any lingering flour into the sink or garbage can.

Chocolate Cake

MAKES TWO 9-INCH CAKES OR 24 CUPCAKES

Another of our most popular basic cakes. As with all chocolate recipes, be sure to use a high-quality cocoa (see page 23).

1½ cups cake flour, plus more for flouring the cake pans
1½ cups sugar, plus more for unmolding the cakes
½ cup (1 stick) unsalted butter, softened at room temperature
⅓ cup unsweetened Dutch-process cocoa powder
1 teaspoon baking soda
¼ teaspoon baking powder
⅓ cup melted unsweetened chocolate (such as Baker's),
*   from two 1-ounce squares*
½ cup hot water
2 extra-large eggs
½ cup buttermilk
Unsalted butter (about 2 tablespoons), nonstick spray
*   or vegetable oil, for greasing the cake pans*

1. Position a rack in the center of the oven, and preheat to 350°F.
2. Put the flour, sugar, butter, cocoa, baking soda, and baking powder in the bowl of a stand mixer fitted with the paddle attachment. (If you don't have a stand mixer, you can use a hand mixer, but take extra care not to over-mix.) Mix on low speed just until the ingredients are blended together, a few seconds, then raise the speed to low-medium and continue to mix until smooth, approximately 1 additional minute.
3. Stop the motor and pour in the chocolate. Mix for 1 minute on low speed. With the motor running, pour in the hot water. Add the eggs, one egg at a time, adding the next one after the previous one has been absorbed. With the motor still running, pour in the buttermilk. Stop the motor periodically and scrape from the bottom with a rubber spatula to be sure all the ingredi-

ents are fully integrated, and return the mixer to low-medium speed. Continue to mix for 1 additional minute to ensure the eggs are fully absorbed. This will also help ensure that all the sugar is dissolved and the flour is thoroughly mixed in, which will help produce a luxurious mouthfeel in the final cake. Before baking, be sure the batter is between 70° and 73°F, or the cake will crown. (If it is too warm, put it in the refrigerator for a few minutes; if too cool, let it rest at room temperature.)

4. Grease two 9-inch cake pans (2 inches deep) and flour them them. (For more, see "To Flour a Cake Pan," page 297.)

5. Divide the batter evenly between the two cake pans, using a rubber spatula to scrape down the bowl and get as much batter as possible out.

6. Bake until the cakes begin to pull from the sides of the pan and are springy to the touch, 25 to 30 minutes.

7. Remove from the oven and let cool for at least 30 minutes, preferably 1 hour. The cakes should be at room temperature before you remove them from the pan. Put a piece of parchment paper on a cookie sheet, sprinkle with sugar, and turn the cakes out onto parchment; the sugar will keep them from sticking.

Refrigerate or freeze (see page 170) until ready to decorate.

White Chiffon Cake

When it comes to chiffon, I am a pure classicist. We only do two things with vanilla chiffon at Carlo's Bake Shop: lemon chiffon and strawberry chiffon (one of my mother's favorites), and those are the only two options you'll find in the chart on page 193.

For this cake, you will need two 7-inch round cake pans (3 inches deep). Note that they should be aluminum, and must *not* be nonstick, or the cakes will collapse while cooling.

2½ cups cake flour
2¼ teaspoons baking powder
¼ teaspoon fine sea salt
1½ cups plus ⅓ cup sugar
6 extra-large eggs, separated
¼ cup vegetable oil
1 teaspoon pure vanilla extract
¾ cup warm water
Distilled white vinegar, for wiping the bowl
1 teaspoon freshly squeezed lemon juice

1. Position a rack in the center of the oven, and preheat to 350°F.
2. Sift together the flour, baking powder, salt, and 1½ cups sugar into the bowl of a stand mixer fitted with the whip attachment. (You can use a hand mixer if you prefer.) Start the mixer slowly to avoid spraying the flour.
3. In a separate bowl, combine the egg yolks, oil, vanilla, and water by hand with a whisk and continue whisking until well mixed.
4. With the motor running on low, pour the egg yolk mixture into the mixer bowl. After 30 seconds, stop and scrape with a rubber spatula. Mix at medium speed until blended together with no lumps, 1 to 1½ minutes.

Transfer the mixture to a clean bowl, using a rubber spatula to scrape down the mixer bowl and get as much batter out as possible.

5. Wash and dry the mixer bowl and whip attachment, then wipe them down with distilled white vinegar to remove all traces of grease and oil. Pour the egg whites and lemon juice into the mixer bowl and start whipping on low speed for about 2 minutes. Slowly add the remaining ⅓ cup sugar and whip on high speed until stiff peaks are formed.

6. With a rubber spatula, fold one third of the meringue into the first mixture. Fold in the remaining meringue in two additions.

7. Gently fill two deep ungreased 7-inch cake pans halfway up.

8. Bake until the sides of the cakes pull away from the pans, 30 to 40 minutes.

9. Remove from the oven and allow to cool. Release the cakes from the pans by flipping them upside down and tapping fiercely against a work surface.

The cakes can be refrigerated in an airtight container for up to 3 days or frozen for up to 2 months.

Chocolate Chiffon

MAKES TWO 10-INCH CAKES

For this cake, you will need two 10-inch Bundt or Bundt-style pans, 3 inches deep. Note that they should be aluminum, and must *not* be nonstick or the cakes will collapse while cooling.

6 extra-large eggs, separated
1½ cups sugar
¾ cup plus 1½ tablespoons cake flour
¾ cup water
½ cup vegetable oil
2½ tablespoons unsweetened Dutch-process cocoa powder
2¼ teaspoons baking powder
1¼ teaspoon fine sea salt
1 teaspoon pure vanilla extract
½ teaspoon baking soda
Distilled white vinegar, for wiping the bowl

1. Position a rack in the center of the oven, and preheat to 350°F.
2. Put the egg yolks, 1 cup of the sugar, the flour, 6 tablespoons of the water, the oil, cocoa, baking powder, salt, vanilla, and baking soda in the bowl of a stand mixer fitted with the whip attachment. (If you don't have a stand mixer, you can use a hand mixer.) Beat starting on low speed, then raise to medium and whip until the mixture is thick and shiny and has multiplied several times in volume, approximately 5 minutes. Pour in the remaining water in a thin stream just until absorbed by the mixture. It will seem watery, but that's okay. Transfer to another bowl and set aside. Wipe out the mixer bowl with vinegar.
3. Put the egg whites in the bowl of the stand mixer and whip for 30 seconds on high speed. With the motor running, add the remaining ½ cup sugar and whip on high until stiff peaks form, 5 to 6 minutes.

4. Fold half the white mixture into the yolk mixture, a little at a time, until uniformly combined. Then pour the combined mixture into the white mixture bowl and fold with a rubber spatula.

6. Do not grease the pans for this recipe. Run some cold water into the pans, rotate them, and shake out the water over the sink. Pour the batter into the pans (it will come about ¾ of the way up the sides), and bake until firm and spongy, 30 to 40 minutes.

7. Remove from the oven and let cool slightly.

8. Manually loosen the cakes by hand from the sides and center tube of the pans, then invert and spank the pan to loosen the cake.

The cakes can be refrigerated in an airtight container for up to 3 days, or may be wrapped in plastic wrap and frozen for up to 2 months.

Pan di Spagna

Italian Sponge Cake

MAKES ONE 9-INCH CAKE

As discussed on page 173, you would never eat this cake without soaking it; it's just too dry on its own. But when you spoon or brush a liqueur or syrup over it, it drinks the liquid in and is transformed. This recipe produces only one cake because, conventionally, you cut this cake in half, usually filling it with a cream infused with the same liqueur you used to soak it. For the most part, you will make this cake with layers of filling that are equal in height to the layers of cake, but if you use a rich filling like Chocolate Ganache (page 318) or Chocolate Fudge Frosting (page 313), use half as much, to keep the filling from overwhelming the cake.

1½ cups sugar, plus more for sprinkling the parchment paper
5 extra-large eggs
1 teaspoon pure vanilla extract
Drop of lemon oil (optional)
1½ cups cake flour, sifted, plus more for flouring the cake pan
⅓ cup vegetable oil
Unsalted butter (about 1 tablespoon), nonstick spray, or vegetable oil, for greasing cake pan

1. Position a rack in the center of the oven, and preheat to 350°F.
2. Put the sugar, eggs, vanilla, and lemon oil (if using) in the bowl of a stand mixer fitted with the whip attachment. (If you don't have a stand mixer, you can use a hand mixer.) Beat starting on low speed and raise to medium. Whip until the mixture is thick, shiny, and ivory in color, and has multiplied several times in volume, approximately 15 minutes. Remove the bowl from the mixer and use a rubber spatula to scrape as much mixture as possible off the whip attachment and into the bowl.

3. Add the flour and patiently fold it in with a rubber spatula. Pour in the oil, and fold in until fully absorbed into the mixture.
4. Grease and flour a 9-inch cake pan pan. (For more, see "To Flour a Cake Pan," page 297.) Pour the batter into the pan, scraping down the sides of the bowl with a rubber spatula.
5. Bake until the cake begins to pull from the sides of the pan and is springy to the touch, 30 to 40 minutes.
6. Remove from the oven and let cool for at least 30 minutes, preferably 1 hour. The cake should be at room temperature before you remove it from the pan.
7. Put a piece of parchment paper on a cookie sheet, sprinkle with sugar, and turn the cake out onto the parchment; the sugar will keep it from sticking.

Refrigerate or freeze (see page 170) until ready to decorate.

Carrot Cake

Golden raisins and walnuts add bursts of sweetness and texture to this classic cake. Note that the carrots carry a lot of moisture, so squeeze out their excess liquid by putting them in a colander and pressing on them with a paper towel after grating to keep the batter from being too wet or loose.

3 cups finely grated carrots (from about 5 large carrots)
2½ cups cake flour, plus more for flouring the cake pans
2 cups sugar, plus more for unmolding the cakes
2 cups Italian Custard Cream (page 315; optional)
¾ cup vegetable oil
2¼ teaspoons baking powder
2 teaspoons ground cinnamon
1 teaspoon baking soda
1 teaspoon pure vanilla extract
½ teaspoon fine sea salt
4 extra-large eggs
1 cup milk
½ cup chopped walnuts
¼ cup golden raisins
Unsalted butter (about 2 tablespoons), nonstick spray,
    or vegetable oil, for greasing the cake pans

1. Position a rack in the center of the oven, and preheat to 350°F.
2. Put the carrots, flour, sugar, custard (if using), oil, baking powder, cinnamon, baking soda, vanilla, and salt in the bowl of a stand mixer fitted with the paddle attachment. (If you don't have a stand mixer, you can use a hand mixer.) Mix on low just until the ingredients are tossed together well, a few seconds, then raise the speed to low-medium and continue to mix until the mixture is smooth, approximately 1 additional minute.

3. With the motor running, add one egg at a time, adding the next one after the previous one has been absorbed. Stop the motor periodically and scrape from the bottom of the bowl with a rubber spatula to incorporate. Return the mixer to low-medium speed.

4. Continue to mix for 1 additional minute to ensure that the eggs are fully absorbed. This will also help ensure that all the sugar is dissolved and the flour is incorporated, which will help produce a luxurious mouthfeel in the final cake.

5. With the motor running, pour in the milk, ½ cup at a time, stopping the motor to scrape the sides and bottom of the bowl between the two additions. Continue to mix for another 1 minute or until the mixture appears smooth. Add the walnuts and raisins and mix just to integrate them.

6. Grease two 9-inch cake pans with the butter, and flour them. (For more, see "To Flour a Cake Pan," page 297.)

7. Divide the batter evenly between the two cake pans, using a rubber spatula to scrape down the bowl and get as much batter as possible out. Before baking, be sure the batter is between 70° and 73°F, or the cakes will crown. (Test by plunging a kitchen thermometer into the center of the batter; if it is too warm, put the bowl in the refrigerator for a few minutes; if too cool, let it rest at room temperature.)

8. Bake until the cake begins to pull from the sides of the pan and is springy to the touch, 25 to 30 minutes.

9. Remove from the oven and let cool for at least 30 minutes, preferably 1 hour. The cake should be at room temperature before you remove it from the pan.

10. Put a piece of parchment paper on a cookie sheet, sprinkle with sugar, and one at a time, turn the pans over and turn the cakes out onto the parchment; the sugar will keep them from sticking.

Refrigerate or freeze (see page 170) until ready to decorate.

Red Velvet Cake

This classic of the American South is just as popular in Hoboken, New Jersey. I never frost this with anything other than Cream Cheese Frosting (page 316).

1¼ cups vegetable shortening
2 cups sugar, plus more for sprinkling the parchment paper
1 tablespoon unsweetened Dutch-process cocoa powder
4½ teaspoons (2 tubes) red food-coloring gel
3 cups cake flour, plus more for flouring the cake pans
1¼ teaspoons fine sea salt
1¼ teaspoons pure vanilla extract
1¼ teaspoons baking soda
1¼ teaspoons distilled white vinegar
3 extra-large eggs
1¼ cups buttermilk
Unsalted butter (about 2 tablespoons), nonstick spray,
    or vegetable oil, for greasing the cake pans

1. Position a rack in the center of the oven, and preheat to 350°F.
2. Put the shortening, sugar, cocoa, food coloring, flour, salt, vanilla, baking soda, and vinegar in the bowl of a stand mixer fitted with the paddle attachment. (You can use a hand mixer if you allow the shortening to soften at room temperature before beginning.) Paddle, starting at low speed, then raise the speed to low-medium and mix for about 1 minute. Add the eggs, one at a time, mixing for 1 minute after each is absorbed into the mixture. Add the buttermilk in two portions, stopping to scrape the sides of the bowl between additions.
3. Grease two 9-inch cake pans (2 inches deep) with the butter, and flour them (see "To Flour a Cake Pan," page 297).

4. Divide the batter evenly between the two cake pans, using a rubber spatula to scrape down the bowl and get as much batter as possible out.
5. Bake until the cakes begin to pull from the sides of the pans and are springy to the touch, 35 to 40 minutes.
6. Remove from the oven and let cool for at least 30 minutes, preferably 1 hour. The cakes should be at room temperature before you remove them from the pan.
7. Put a piece of parchment paper on a cookie sheet, sprinkle with sugar, and one at a time, turn the pans over and turn the cakes out onto the parchment; the sugar will keep them from sticking.

Refrigerate or freeze (see page 170) until ready to decorate.

Frostings and Fillings

Vanilla Frosting

MAKES ABOUT 4 CUPS, ENOUGH TO FILL AND ICE ONE 9-INCH CAKE

For a creamier frosting, use milk instead of water. You must refrigerate this frosting, as well as any cakes filled or iced with it. Let it come to room temperature before using, and whisk briefly by hand to refresh it.

> *2½ cups (5 sticks) unsalted butter, softened*
> *5 cups powdered (10X) sugar*
> *1 tablespoon pure vanilla extract*
> *¼ teaspoon fine sea salt*
> *3 tablespoons lukewarm water*

1. Put the butter in the bowl of a stand mixer fitted with the paddle attachment and mix on low speed until butter is smooth with no lumps. With the motor running, add the sugar, 1 cup at a time, adding the next cup only after the first addition has been integrated into the mixture.
2. Stop the machine and add the vanilla and salt. Paddle on low-medium speed until completely smooth, approximately 2 minutes. Add the water and continue to mix until light and fluffy, 2 to 3 minutes.

The frosting can be kept in an airtight container at room temperature for up to 2 days.

Chocolate Fudge Frosting

For a creamier frosting, use milk instead of water. You must refrigerate this frosting, as well as any cakes filled or iced with it. Let it come to room temperature before using, and whisk briefly by hand to refresh it.

2½ cups (5 sticks) unsalted butter, softened
5 cups powdered (10X) sugar
⅔ cup unsweetened Dutch-process cocoa powder
1 tablespoon pure vanilla extract
¼ teaspoon fine sea salt
3 tablespoons lukewarm water

1. Put the butter in the bowl of a stand mixer fitted with the paddle attachment and paddle on low speed until smooth, with no lumps, approximately 3 minutes. With the motor running, add the sugar, one cup at a time, adding the next cup only after the first addition is absorbed.
2. Stop the machine and add the cocoa, vanilla, and salt. Paddle on low-medium speed until completely smooth, approximately 2 minutes. Add the water and continue to paddle until light and fluffy, 2 to 3 minutes.

The frosting will keep for up to 2 days in an airtight container at room temperature.

Italian Buttercream

MAKES ABOUT 7 CUPS

I adapted this recipe from one used at The Culinary Institute of America, shown to me by a group of students for whom I did a demonstration.

8 extra-large egg whites
2 cups sugar
½ cup water
4 cups (8 sticks) unsalted butter, at room temperature, cut into small cubes
1 tablespoon pure vanilla extract

1. Put the whites in the bowl of a stand mixer fitted with the whip attachment.
2. Put 1½ cups of the sugar and the water in a heavy saucepan and bring to a boil over medium-high heat, stirring with a wooden spoon to dissolve the sugar. Continue to cook, without stirring, and bring to the soft ball stage (240°F).
3. Meanwhile, whip the whites at high speed until soft peaks form, approximately 5 minutes. With the motor running, add the remaining ½ cup sugar gradually, continuing to whip until medium peaks form.
4. When the sugar reaches 240°F, with the motor running, pour it into the egg whites, very slowly, in a thin stream, to avoid cooking the eggs. Raise the speed to high, and continue to whip until the mixture has cooled to room temperature, 10 to 15 minutes.
5. Stopping the motor between additions, add the butter in 5 increments, scraping the bowl with a rubber spatula before adding each addition of butter. With the motor running, add the vanilla, and whip just until it is blended in.

The buttercream can be refrigerated in an airtight container for up to 1 week. Let it come to room temperature and paddle briefly before using.

Italian Custard Cream

The longer you cook this cream, the thicker it will become, so you can—and should—adjust the texture to suit your taste.

2½ cups whole milk
1 tablespoon pure vanilla extract
1 cup sugar
⅔ cup cake flour, sifted
5 extra-large egg yolks
2 teaspoons salted butter

1. Put the milk and vanilla in a saucepan and bring to a simmer over medium heat.
2. In a bowl, whip together the sugar, flour, and egg yolks with a hand mixer. Ladle a cup of the milk-vanilla mixture into the bowl and beat to temper the yolks.
3. Add the yolk mixture to the pot and beat over medium heat with the hand mixer until thick and creamy, about 1 minute. As you are beating, move the pot on and off the flame so that you don't scramble the eggs.
4. Remove the pot from the heat, add the butter, and whip for 2 minutes to thicken the cream. Transfer to a bowl. Let cool, cover with plastic wrap, and refrigerate at least 6 hours.

Will keep for up to 1 week.

To make chocolate custard cream, add 1½ ounces melted, cooled unsweetened chocolate along with the butter. For a richer chocolate flavor, add a little more.

Cream Cheese Frosting

MAKES ABOUT 3 CUPS, ENOUGH TO FILL AND ICE ONE 9-INCH CAKE

I always make this frosting—the classic filling and topping for Carrot Cake (page 306) and Red Velvet Cake (page 308)—with Philadelphia brand cream cheese, which I think is simply the best. Use this as soon as you make it because it gets very stiff in the refrigerator. If you have to refrigerate it, do not microwave it to freshen it. Instead, let it rest at room temperature for 4 hours to soften.

Two 8-ounce packages cream cheese
½ cup (1 stick) unsalted butter, softened
1 teaspoon pure vanilla extract
2 cups powdered (10X) sugar, sifted

1. Put the cream cheese and butter in the bowl of a stand mixer fitted with the paddle attachment and paddle at medium speed until creamy, approximately 30 seconds.
2. With the motor running, pour in the vanilla and paddle for 30 seconds. Add the sugar, a little at a time, and mix until smooth, approximately 1 minute after the last addition.

Use right away, or refrigerate in an airtight container for up to 2 days.

My Dad's Chocolate Mousse

MAKES ABOUT 3½ CUPS, ENOUGH TO FILL AND ICE ONE 9-INCH CAKE

This chocolate whipped cream, which we still make with my Dad's recipe, is fluffy and rich, and gets along with a wide range of cakes and fillings.

2 cups heavy cream
½ cup sugar
3 tablespoons unsweetened Dutch-process cocoa powder
1 tablespoon Kahlúa or coffee liqueur

Put the cream, sugar, cocoa powder, and Kahlúa in a stainless-steel mixing bowl. Blend with a hand mixer at high speed until fluffy, about 1 minute.

Use immediately or refrigerate in an airtight container for up to 3 days.

Chocolate Ganache

MAKES ABOUT 2 CUPS

This ganache can be used as a filling and/or poured over a cake. To use it as a filling, refrigerate it, transfer it to a pastry bag, and pipe it out following the directions on page 172.

To pour ganache over a cake, melt it in a double boiler and simply pour it over a cake or layer. To top layers of French cream or chocolate mousse with ganache, pour it on and smooth it with a cake icing spatula.

1 cup heavy cream
9 ounces semisweet chocolate, coarsely chopped
1 tablespoon light corn syrup

1. Put the heavy cream in a saucepan and set it over medium-high heat. As soon as it begins to simmer, remove the pot from the heat. Add the chocolate and stir with a wooden spoon to melt the chocolate. Stir in the corn syrup.

2. To cover a cake with poured ganache, set a wire rack in or over a baking tray. Set the cake on the rack. Carefully ladle the molten ganache over the cake in a steady stream, letting it run over the cake until uniformly covered.

3. Otherwise, transfer to a bowl and refrigerate for about 1 hour. If using for filling, soften in a double boiler over medium heat until pourable.

4. Let any unused ganache cool, transfer to an airtight container, and refrigerate for up to 3 days. Reheat gently in a double boiler set over simmering water, stirring with a rubber spatula until warm and pourable.

Lobster Tail Cream

MAKES 5½ CUPS

We use this decadent cream to fill our signature lobster tail pastries, but it can also be used to fill and/or frost cakes; it's especially delicious on our Vanilla Cake (page 296).

The amount of Bailey's Irish Cream is negligible, but it adds a subtle elegance.

Italian Custard Cream (page 315)
Italian Whipped Cream (page 321)
2 tablespoons Bailey's Irish Cream liqueur,
   plus more to taste (optional)

1. Put the custard cream in a mixing bowl. Add the whipped cream, a little at a time, folding it in with a rubber spatula.
2. Drizzle the Bailey's Irish Cream (if using), over the mixture, gently mixing it in. Add more to taste, if desired, but do not overmix the cream.

The cream can be refrigerated in an airtight container for up to 4 days. Whisk briefly by hand to refresh before using.

Italian Whipped Cream

MAKES ABOUT 2½ CUPS

This sweetened whipped cream can be used to fill and/or ice cakes, and is also a component of French cream and lobster cream.

1½ cups heavy cream
¼ cup plus 2 tablespoons sugar

Put the cream and sugar in a bowl and whip on high speed with a hand mixer. Do not overmix or you'll end up with butter.

The cream can be refrigerated in an airtight container for up to 3 days. Whisk by hand to refresh before using.

Syrup

Use this recipe to make syrups to soak the sponge cake on page 304. In addition to the liqueurs called for in the book, you can use the formula to create other syrups. A good rule of thumb for selecting a brand of liqueur is to pick what you like to drink, and steer clear of the cheap stuff.

For a stronger flavor, increase the amount of liqueur up to ½ cup.

1 cup water
1 cup sugar
¼ cup liqueur, such as Rosolio, Strega, or rum (see Note below)

Put the water, sugar, and liqueur into a saucepan and bring to a simmer over medium-high heat. Whisk until the sugar dissolves, approximately 3 to 4 minutes. Let cool before using.

The syrup may be refrigerated in an airtight container for up to 2 weeks.

Note: Rosolio and Strega can be hard to find. There is no truly comparable replacement for them, but you can substitute other sweet liqueurs if you cannot get your hands on them.

Acknowledgments

Nobody writes a book by himself, and I'd like to thank the following people for their help on this project, and in the growing family of *Cake Boss* shows:

My wife, Lisa. Thank you for sharing all the great adventures with me, both the wonderful and wild ride we've enjoyed with *Cake Boss*, and the even greater adventure of Life. There's nobody I'd rather have as my partner through it all. I love you.

My Sofia Bear, Buddy, Marco, and Carlo—my four incredible kids. You guys make me proud every day, and continue to be my inspiration—you're why I get out of bed and go to work every morning, and the reason I can't wait to come home at the end of the day.

My father, Buddy Valastro, the original Cake Boss. As it says on that picture in our bakery, you may be gone, but you are not forgotten. We all miss you, and work to honor you every day of our lives.

Mary Valastro (Mama). You may not be as involved with Carlo's Bake Shop as you used to be, but your presence is still felt there every minute of every day, and the personal and professional examples you set will guide me always.

My four big sisters, Grace, Madeline, Mary, and Lisa. It's tough to put words to how much I care about the four of you. You've been there, literally, my entire life and I love knowing you're there, in my corner, every day of the year.

My brothers-in-law, Mauro, Joey, and Joe. You guys will always be like the brothers I never had. As far as I'm concerned, we should just drop the "in-law"— you're my real brothers. I have to also give tremendous, special thanks to Joey for testing the recipes for this book—and in his own home kitchen, no less. (I don't know how he talked my sister Grace into letting him do that, but I was impressed that he did!)

The crew at the bakery for helping the place run like a well-oiled machine, especially Frankie and Danny, and special thanks to Frankie, Liz, Rachael, and Melanie for their help with the photo shoots for this book. Also, a huge appreciative shout-out to German for helping with the recipe testing.

Adam Bourcier, thanks for all the help on the book, and for continuing to help manage this empire's growth. We've got big things on the horizon and I'm happy to have you on the team.

Nikky O'Connell, my personal assistant. You do so much, and I appreciate all of it. I couldn't accomplish what I do without you.

Sal Picinich. A lot of the wisdom in this book I learned from you. I miss you, but I'm comforted to know that you're in heaven, baking with my dad.

Andrew Friedman. Once again, you've taken my thoughts and magically transferred them to the page. I'm happy to call you my friend.

Marcus Nilsson, thanks for your great photography and for being a pleasure to work with on those long shoot days. To Stephanie Hanes for her lovely prop styling. And to Bridget Stoyko, Melissa Stonehill, and Tracy Collins for their expert production and management of the photo shoots.

The team at my publisher, Free Press: our editor, Leslie Meredith, for her continued support and encouragement; publisher Martha Levin for her abiding belief; editorial assistant Donna Loffredo for her help during the editing and production stage; VP director of publicity Carisa Hays, for getting the word out. And to editorial director Dominick Anfuso and associate publisher Suzanne Donahue for their very special support of this project.

Jon Rosen and the team at William Morris Endeavor Entertainment. Thanks for a truly fantastic year; can't wait to see what we pull off next!

Erin Niumata of Folio Literary Management, who agented this book—thanks for your friendship and for making this project happen the right way. And my lasting appreciation to Maura Teitelbaum at Abrams Artists Agency for her early direction and guidance.

The Brooks Group, Carlo's Bake Shop's public relations agency—thanks for getting the word out about all the exciting news we've had over the last year, and for your terrific advice and enthusiasm along the way.

To my extended family—my aunts and uncles, cousins and second cousins—and to all my friends (you know who you are), thanks for everything and for helping me stay grounded during these life-changing couple of years.

The loyal customers of Carlo's Bake Shop—thanks for lining up to visit us, and for all the enthusiasm you bring to our shop. When we bake and decorate, we think of you and how much pleasure we hope our products bring to you.

I have to also thank God, for giving me a blessed life—my family and our business would have been riches enough for any man; all the rest is just the icing on the cake.

And to the rest of my extended family at TLC and Discovery: David Zaslav, president and CEO, Discovery Communications; Eileen O'Neill, group president, Discovery and TLC Networks; Joe Abruzzese, president, Advertising Sales,

US Networks; Nancy Daniels, EVP, Production and Development, Discovery Channel; Howard Lee, SVP, Production and Development, TLC; Dustin Smith, VP, Communications, TLC; Sue Perez-Jackson, director, Licensing, Discovery Communications; Edward Sabin, group COO, Discovery and TLC Networks; and Jen Williams, VP, Talent Management and Strategy. And two essential figures who no longer work on the show, but who helped shape it and its success: John Paul Stoops and Jon Sechrist. I love working with all of you. Thank you for helping me realize my dreams and for all we have achieved together, and will continue to achieve in the future.

To my fans. Without you guys, I wouldn't be the Cake Boss. Thanks for watching, for writing, for coming to the live shows, and for buying my books. You're the best and I love you all.

Index

Note: Page references in *italics* indicate photographs.

D

daisy cupcakes, 162, *162*
decorating techniques
    applying fondant to cake, 201–2
    assembling pastries and cakes, 100
    basics for working with fondant, 196
    creating "feathered" icing, 95
    for cupcakes, 158
    "dirty-icing" cakes (crumb-coating),
        155, 197
    dusting doughnuts with sugar, 118
    establishing front and back of cake,
        186
    estimating buttercream quantities,
        155
    filling cakes, 171
    freezing cakes before decorating,
        170–71
    freezing cookies before frosting, 81
    icing a cake with poster board, 198
    icing (frosting) cakes, 172–73
    making a parchment pencil, 185–86
    ratios of filling to cake, 172
    rolling out fondant, 199–200
    saving pastry bags, 197
    trimming and cutting cakes, 170–71
    using a decorator's comb, 184
    working with icing, 81, 95, 172–73,
        184, 198
    see also piping techniques
decorator's buttercream, 154
decorator's comb, using, 184
devil's food cake, vanilla, 191
"dirty-icing" cakes (crumb-coating), 155,
    197
docking technique, 94
doily-lined cardboard circle, 203
dot and bow cake, *204,* 205–7
dots, piped, 174, 175, 176
double boilers, 15
double reverse loop, piped, 174, 176

doughnuts
    dusting, with cinnamon sugar, 118
    old-fashioned, 115–19, *116*
    shapes for, 119
Dragone, Danny, 5
droplines, piped, 178, 180

E

Easter basket, *222,* 223–25
éclair dough, 88
éclairs, 89–91
egg(s)
    notes about, 25
    whites, whipped, folding, 98
    whites, whipping, 56
equipment
    all purpose cookware, 13–15
    baking pans and trays, 13
    for cakes and cupcakes, 15–16
    cookie sheets, 15
    double boilers, 15
    mini muffin trays, 15
    pie pans, 15
    storage for, 12
    see also tools

F

Father's day cake, *238,* 239–41
Faugno, Joey, 5, 49
filigree, piped, 179, 180
fillings
    applying to cakes, 171
    cannoli cream, 109
    chocolate ganache, 318–19
    estimating quantities for cakes,
        172
    Italian custard cream, 315
    Italian whipped cream, 321

Buddy Valastro is an accomplished fourth-generation baker born in Hoboken, New Jersey. At an early age, it was clear that he was a natural baker and would go into the family business. He loved spending time with his father, a master baker, as an apprentice working for countless hours in the bakery learning the Old World secrets of baking. They dreamed that together they would make Carlo's Bake Shop a household name. Since his father's passing when Buddy was seventeen, and with the help of his family, his father's recipes, and his own innovative decorating and sugar art techniques, Buddy has taken Carlo's Bake Shop to new heights.

Today, Buddy is often asked to demonstrate, compete, and teach his craft around the country. At Carlo's, Buddy and his staff turn out thousands of wedding cakes, specialty cakes, and pastries weekly. His award-winning designs have been featured numerous times in different bridal and baking magazines. His memoir cookbook, *Cake Boss: The Stories and Recipes from Mia Famiglia*, was a *New York Times* bestseller and Carlo's Bake Shop has been featured in books, newspapers such as the *New York Times*, and television, mostly TLC's hit *Cake Boss*. He and his cakes have also been featured on the *Today* show, *Good Morning America*, *The View*, and HBO's hit series *The Sopranos*.